The Lost of Parkwood Springs

A collection of treasured memories

By Barbara Warsop

Past residents of Parkwood Springs
2014 Reunion meeting at Hillsborough Hotel, Langsett Rd.
L to R back row: Roy Smith, Allan Cottingham, Ray Swift, Eric Boocock, David Young.
L to R Middle row: Barry Robinson, Terry Turner, Roger Simcox, Lynn Young, David Peacock, Tony Lamb.
L to R Front row: Pat Woodhouse, Barbara Lee, Barbara Warsop, Maureen Hunter, Eileen Taylor and George Hunter seated.

Text copyright 2017 © Barbara Warsop

The rights of Barbara Warsop and her work have been asserted by her in accordance with the Copyright, Design Patent Act 1988

April 2017   ISBN: 978-1-906722-49-4

Parkwood Springs Group
2016
Preface

This book is in memory of all the people who lived on Parkwood Springs, Military Personal who died during WWI/WWII, and those who lost their lives during the blitz of 1940 when a bomb dropped at the bottom of Pickering Rd, and for the people who tried to make things better during the upheaval of the slum clearance.

For some time I had searched for something written; books or photos of the Parkwood Springs village community prior to the slum clearances of 1973. Most information I found was sporadic and on the internet.

Pat Woodhouse, a past resident of Parkwood Springs, was looking for pictures of Parkwood Springs at Stannington Festival (Art Exhibition) where we met up by coincidence in 2014. We chatted about the lack of information on Parkwood Springs. So I took the decision to try and put something together on the subject, photos, stories, etc with a view to publishing something.

I placed an article in the Sheffield Star RETRO to ask for past Parkwood Springs residents to contact me. Twenty people responded and I organised a reunion.
Here is a collection of those stories. I am sure there are many more stories to be told.
With apologies to all Parkwood Springer's who do not appear in this book.

Some friendships formed on Parkwood Springs have lasted a lifetime and some former residents continue to meet up for reunions and to reminisce about their time living there and what a wonderful community it once was.
I felt it was important to capture some of these stories before they are forgotten.

Many people, especially those who are new to Sheffield, are unaware that there used to be a whole community of people living on Parkwood Springs in the past.
Parkwood Springs Group is made up of people who are mostly retired, many of us over 70 years of age. These memories needed recording before they are lost forever.

When I set out to write the book of people's lives on Parkwood Springs and the wonderful community spirit that existed among us.
What I found remarkable and interesting was the fact that we are all in our own way saying the same thing
Parkwood Springs was a lovely place to live and be a part of.

CONTENTS

A Short history of Parkwood Springs Housing Circa 1850

Originally the land of "Old Parkwood" was a deer park and hunting ground, part of the Duke of Norfolk's Estate.
Two miles of land between Owlerton Wards End in the north & Neepsend in the south & east of the river Don rose steeply from 200 feet to 575 feet above sea level.

By 1845 Parkwood was severed from Neepsend by the Manchester, Sheffield and Lincolnshire Railway line. The Bardwell Road Bridge was built in 1848 and served as the only entrance to "Old Parkwood" it was designed by Sir John Fowler born in Wadsley. Fowler was an engineer on the Forth Road Bridge.
(Courtesy of Sheffield Archaeology Students of Sheffield University)

According to Paul Hodkinson's book "A History of Neepsend"

In 1850 the Parkwood Springs Land and Building Society purchased 27 acres adjoining the Old Parkwood and railway and divided it into 95 allotments of 500 to 1200 yards
By 1861 upon these freehold allotments, Parkwood Springs had 171 houses and a population of 792. On the highest parts the houses had magnificent views towards Rivelin, Loxley and Bradfield moors.

The ordnance survey map of 1863 shows the allotments with detached houses surrounded by large gardens and the wood on the hill. The road names differing from present day, Orchard Rd, Prospect Rd, Mount Rd, Vale Rd and Norfolk Roads date from 1856.

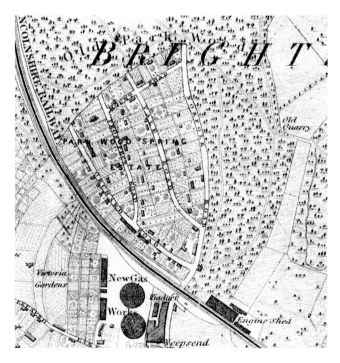

Norfolk Road was named after the Duke of Norfolk owner of the Old Parkwood.
Was renamed Norfolk Rd North. However there was another Norfolk Road in Sheffield.
To avoid confusion it was renamed Douglas Road.
Orchard Road became Wallace Road; Prospect Road became Pickering Road. The 1873
Ordnance Survey map shows the road name changes that had taken place.

Joseph Pickering of (Joseph Pickering and Sons LTD) founder of Parkwood Springs Land
Society was Church Warden of St Michaels and All Angels, Neepsend. In 1860 he built a
house on Vale Rd. Later he became Councillor for Sharrow Ward and bought a house
there. Prospect Rd was renamed Pickering Rd in honour of Councillor Joseph Pickering.

In 1864 there was an industrial belt running through Neepsend to the river Don and the
Private Rd from the railway bridge to Neepsend shown on the 1851 Ordnance Survey
map was abandoned, and a new more direct road, Bardwell Road, was constructed to
link the Parkwood Spring Estate to Neepsend.

1866-1875 lots of factories were growing all around the Neepsend area.
A Beer house was built at the bottom of Douglas Road.
Building continued on the Parkwood Springs Estate. Brick terraced houses were built
along parts of Wallace Road and Mount Road and two short blocks on Douglas Road.

A new road was made in 1873 from Neepsend Lane up towards the railway this was
called Parkwood Road. The Gas works had expanded towards the new road to cope with
an increased demand. About 1870 gas was first used in cooking.
During 1873 to 1890 changes took place on Parkwood Springs and a small quarry and
brick works were built where woodland had once been between the bottom of Douglas
Rd and Rutland Rd by the side of the engine sheds belonging to the railway. To the north
of Parkwood Springs another patch of woodland was cleared for more quarry workings.
Above the estate a piece of land was cleared and grassed for recreational purposes.
During this time more building took place and the once very middle class estate now had
rows of back to back and terraced houses. They were heavily polluted by the gas works,
steel works and the railway.

As the railway line continued from Manchester, the people who were building the rail line
moved into accommodation near to where they were working. So railway workers came
to live on Parkwood Springs many from Ireland. Eventually about 700 or more people
who worked on the railway came to live on Parkwood Springs. Almost all the houses on
Wallace Road belonged to the railway to house their workers.
One story by a rail worker said as they dug to build the sidings for the rail line they were
finding bodies, this must have been part of the old Wards End Cemetery that exists on
both sides of the rail line.

Neepsend station was completed and opened on 14th July 1888 to serve the industry
with two platforms on the Woodhead line which connected to Sheffield Victoria &
Manchester London Road.
It closed on 28th October 1940 due to low public usage.

Footbridge, Neepsend Station circa 1900

Neepsend Footbridge 2015

With further developments on the Railway a foot bridge was built over the railway line and steps leading to the houses on Wallace Rd, and a genel up the hill to the top of Pickering Rd.

By the early twentieth Century the houses were of a very diverse nature, and great swathes of trees on the Old Parkwood disappeared following an agreement with the Duke of Norfolk`s estate to tip ash from the power station at Neepsend in the area formerly covered by woodland. The tipped ash was dispatched from the gas works to the former woodland by aerial ropeway (cable car.)

1938 the Ganister Mine Opened.
Ganister is a close-grained hard siliceous stone found in the lower coal-measures of South Yorkshire and used for furnace linings. It was a drift mine, the shaft driven horizontally into the hillside. It was described as a happy pit because there were no falls, accidents or labour trouble.

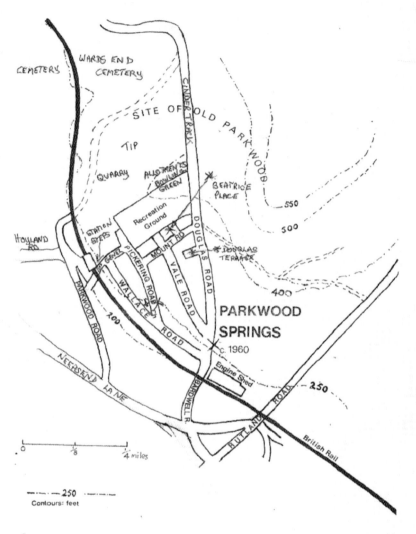

CEMETERY

WARDS END CEMETERY

SITE OF OLD PARKWOOD

CINDER TRACK

TIP

QUARRY

ALLOTMENTS

BOWLING GREEN

BEATRICE PLACE

Recreation Ground

550

500

STATION STEPS

HOYLAND RD

GENE

PICKERING ROAD

MOUNT RD

DOUGLAS ROAD

VALE ROAD

DOUGLAS TERRACE

WALLACE ROAD

PARKWOOD ROAD

400

NEEPSEND LANE

PARKWOOD

SPRINGS

c. 1960

Engine Shed

BRADWELL R

RUTLAND ROAD

250

British Rail

0   ⅛   ¼ miles

----- 250 -----
Contours: feet

6

ROCK HOUSE
51 Pickering Road

On the estate was a very large house called "Rock House" with landscaped garden, shrubbery, lawns, fountain, greenhouse, flowerbeds and kitchen garden.

The "The Castle House" was originally a folly built in the large garden by the owner of "Rock House.
There was an underground passageway connecting the two Buildings.

Circa: 1871 Henry Mills Barlow. Cutler Manufacturer lived at "Rock House"
51 Prospect Road, Parkwood Springs
Well known for the famous "Barlow Pocket Knife".
(Prospect Rd, Later named Pickering Rd)

By 1925 they had become two very large separate houses.
Mr Frank Lacey (Builder) lived in one house and Benjamin Stow (Butcher) lived in the other. Both Rock House and Castle House had the same address of 51 Pickering Road. Both houses have had many tenants over the years.

Castle House and below Puttergill's paper shop 65 Pickering Rd.

"Artist's impression" by Barbara Warsop.

1920`s Onwards

The Houses of Parkwood Springs were situated in a unique space between the Sheffield to Manchester railway line. The Gas Works on Parkwood Road Neepsend, a quarry, ganister mine, Hallamshire Steel and File Co, and the Neepsend locomotive sheds.

At the top of the hill there was the recreation ground, allotments a bowling green and the tip- Now named Viridor Land fill site. To be closed 2020. We thought the allotments and the Bowling Green were the best in Sheffield, with wonderful views of Sheffield.

The only access being a low, narrow Railway Arch on Bardwell Road, which remains the same today.
The only other way to access Parkwood Springs was on foot. There was a cinder track from Douglas Rd to Herries Road, a track to Rutland Road and Cooks Wood Road, Shireclife. (Cinders were the ash from the power station) And the foot bridge over the railway line from Parkwood Road Neepsend.

Just a mile from Sheffield City Centre It was cut off from the rest of Sheffield by the very nature of the place. A true village. Whole families lived there, three and four generations. We had most of what we needed without travelling far.

There were three public houses, two next door to one another at the bottom of Douglas road (The Parkwood Hotel, owned by Whitbread Brewery) & The Reindeer Inn (originally the beer house.) where steel workers used to quench their thirst, after a tough day working in the hot environment of the rolling mill at the Hallamshire Steel and File Company on Bardwell Road.
Another pub was at the top of Douglas Rd the "Douglas Inn" known locally as the top house.
There was a Beer off (off licence) on Mount Road, news agents on Pickering Rd, two chip shops, one on Mount Rd and one just under the arch at the bottom of Douglas Rd, a grocers shop on every road, a cobblers, and two hair dressers.
And GW Waugh LTD mineral water manufacturers Douglas Rd.

Two public telephone boxes were the only form of communication for the whole community at that time. Only business people would have a phone.

There was a Methodist Chapel and the new prefabricated church of St Michaels and All Angels.
The nearest public transport was the old Sheffield to Wadsley Bridge tram on Neepsend Lane. Only a very few people had a car before the 1950`s.

Many residents worked at the gas works, Hallamshire Steel works, the railway, cutlery plus many more factories in Sheffield.
In fact we helped to keep Sheffield on the map and running during the wartime with many working in reserved occupations like railways and steel works.
There was a man that we called an onion Johnny who came once a year from abroad. On his bicycle his beret on his head selling his onions all hanging on raffia string from his bicycle.

Coal Lorries were the only vehicles to come up Parkwood as large vehicles could not get under the railway arch.

A rag and bone man came with his horse and cart shouting" Donkey Stone for rags".
Or he would exchange wooden pegs or a balloon for your rags.
Donkey stone was used to whiten the edge of outside steps, Women were proud of their outside step after they were scrubbed and whitened.

Sometimes a gypsy came around selling their wares door to door. It could have been flowers (Chrysanthemums) they made from shreds of wood and pegs.

The last of the Parkwood forest was felled during the 1926 general strike for firewood.

Artist's impression by B Warsop
Top left: Mount Rd looking towards Pickering Rd
Top Right: Railway Arch Douglas Rd with Wallace Rd on the right
Bottom: Douglas Rd with the wood on the Left

Drawn from the film "Wings of Mystery – 1963"

Barbara Warsop (nee Eadon)

I was born in 1938 at 82 Pickering Rd and lived there for 26 years until I married in 1964.
Our House was semi detached and had two bedrooms a kitchen/dining room and front room with two cellars and an attic. Our outside toilet, was a midden (earth closet) until after the war when we had water laid on, a zinc bath hung on wall outside.
A black lead range fireplace was for heat and cooking. There was a fireplace in all the rooms but we only lit the fire in the bed rooms if we were ill or in the front room if we had company.
Our house stood on a raised piece of land above the other houses on Pickering Rd with wonderful views of the surrounding area of Sheffield, and a very large garden.
It had originally been the police house.

My father Alfred Eadon was born on Wallace Rd in 1908.
He had three brothers and a sister. His father died very young 29 years old. 1911
With no husband grandma had to take in washing to put food on the table for her family. She was also called upon by neighbours to help deliver babies or with someone who had passed away.
Later she married Mr Page and two more brothers were born Lewis and then Douglas. Douglas died at the age of 16 years on 18-1-1938.
Dad and 3 of his brothers, Joseph, Edward, and Lewis, all moved into houses on Parkwood Springs after marriage. Joe lived on Mount Rd, Edward on Pickering Rd, and Lewis lived on Wallace Rd in the same yard as grandma.
Sister Lillian and Brother John moved off Parkwood when they married.

Dad met my mother, Mary Walker at St Michaels and All Angels church on Neepsend and they married there in 1936 and rented our house from Mr Weston a private landlord.

Dad sang in the choir at St Michaels he was also a church warden.
Mum and dad were both members of St Michael's operatic society.
Dad being a tenor taking the lead in many a production of Gilbert and Sullivan and others, mum a soprano in the chorus.

My Father worked at Rawson's Brewery in Town, which became Duncan Gilmour & Co ltd (famous for Gilmour's Windsor Ales) before he was called up to serve his country in 1940.
He was a cook in the Royal Army Catering Core and was stationed in Belgium.
When he got demobbed he was a driver for Tetley's Brewery.

Mum worked at Joseph Pickering and Sons Ltd Burton Road, Neepsend. They produced Blanco (A White Polish Widely used for military and sportsman)

1939 just Before Dad was called up he built us an" Anderson" air raid shelter in the garden. It was half buried corrugated iron structure and grass covered so it couldn't be seen from above. Just big enough to take 4 people, It had a bunk bed and seats and I remember being taken from my bed during the night and mum dressing me in a siren suit (an all in one garment) and carrying me down the garden path to the shelter, then being tucked up in this bunk bed.
Mum was always up before the sirens went off. She had heard the drones of the German planes many miles away and was terrified that a bomb would drop on the gas tanks.

I hardly knew my Dad I was a baby when he left and a 7 year old when he returned after the war.

After Dad left my grandma on mums side and mums Sister Doris came to live with us for moral support for the period of the war. Grandma died at our house during that time.

Aunt Doris never went back to their house on Reginald St.

Lives changed during the war but we as children never noticed and carried on playing.

A bomb dropped at the corner of Pickering and Wallace Rd, which blew out our window. A lump of shrapnel just missed Aunt Doris head, which could have killed her.

I started Hillfoot County School when I was 5 years old. 1943.

I wore a blouse and navy blue gymslip over vest and liberty bodice and navy blue knickers.

I always had a bad chest and a snotty nose. I carried a hanky up my knickers leg.

This was a flour bag that mum unpicked and boiled to take out the starch, which made it nice and soft. (Flour was bought in cotton bags that were starched to hold in the flour.)

Because the war was on we all had to take our gas masks to school. I remember the day our headmaster organised an exercise in the schoolyard with all the children. To make sure we all knew how to put on our gas masks in case of an emergency.

He said, "When I blow my whistle you must all put your gas masks on"

Because I was small at only five years old my mask was a full head mask and I couldn't get it on. I thought the gas was real and started to scream. Then I heard Mr Simmons our head teacher say, "Someone help that child, "and an older girl came to my rescue.

My recycling days began then, jam jars were taken to school for recycling.

I remember the iron railings being taken off peoples outside garden walls for the war effort. Beer and pop bottles were retuned to get your deposit back. Boys called round the houses to see if you wanted your empty bottles taking back and they would get the cash. It would only be a few pence.

Our Doctors surgery was on Penistone Road. He had one room for consultation and another for dispensing medicine. We had to wait to be seen and again for our medicine to be mixed for us, both to be paid for. Pre NHS. We only went to our Doctor if it was necessary. All on foot a fare trek from the top of the hill if you were feeling poorly.

Coal was our only source of heat, no hot water, or electricity. Our lighting was gas mantles on the wall, a very dull light. Mum and dad had to pay for electricity to be installed in 1948 when I was 10 years old.

To get to the Tram stop on Neepsend Lane we had to pass the Hallamshire steel and file co. During the 1940`s steel was delivered by horse and dray and in every entrance there would be four very large shire horses tethered to a dray getting fed up of waiting to be loaded with the steel billets, stamping and snorting and in winter steam would be coming from there nostrils. I was terrified of them, as they towered above me, thinking they would kick me as I passed by them. If there were no horses we saw the red hot steel billets going in and out, back and forth through the rolling mill getting smaller and smaller. The men would be wielding the billets with large tongs and wore white mufflers (scarf's) around their necks to wipe the sweat away.

In the 1940s Mr Torry the local Joiner who lived in a big house at the top of Pickering

Road, had a workshop in a large garage that was positioned between the houses on Wallace Road and Pickering Road the entrance being on Pickering Road. After the war he made me a scooter and a dolls house out of recycled tea chests my dad acquired from the brewery, we still had rationing then and wood hard to come by.

At the "The Gas Works", on Parkwood Road there were four gas tanks below our houses and sulphur coated our windows with a blue film, so our windows had to be cleaned regularly. We never noticed the pollution it was an everyday occurrence.
During the war coke was sold by the gas company to replace the shortage of coal.
We had to queue at the gate on Parkwood Rd to pay for a sack of coke, which was weighed while you waited, or paid to collect an empty sack to pick your own from the Gas tip (slag heap) at the top of the hill. I remember the large queues. Everyone with their own make shift carrier e.g., wheel barrows or prams or anything home made with wheels on, (just like a Lowry Painting.) If we bought a sack we had to walk up the hill to the ash tip, to pick our own coke. It was a filthy job lying among the ash to try and get some good large pieces and then getting it home, very tiring dirty work. All this was done with a community spirit of the time. When we lit the fire with the Coke we would hope we had not got a clinker in it, because a hot a clinker would fly out of the fire like a firework and set light to the peg rug if you were not quick enough to move it.
(Coke is once heated coal, and a clinker was the residue left from the industrial coking process).

At the bottom of Bardwell road was a Pawn Shop. Well used by all to buy or pawn anything for cash. Most of us were poor and things were hard to get during the war time. I remember taking our radio accumulators (Rechargeable electric cell) there to be charged up. They were 4" x 10" tall square glass bottles, very heavy and full of acid.

If Mum saw the gypsy coming selling their wares she would hide on the cellar steps. This was after one had put a curse on her because she didn't want to buy anything. The gypsy went away waving her arms shouting *"curse on you, curse on you,"* all down our path.
We had a very large garden with beautiful lilac trees either side of a big wooden gate between the large wall which separated us from the road. There was a pear tree, laburnum tree, hawthorn hedges and blue lupin which still grow at the top of Parkwood springs today. After the war, dad built a large greenhouse where he grew tomatoes in summer and chrysanthemums in winter which he gave away. We kept chickens, rabbits and he even brought home a goat, straight into the house. Mam shouted get that thing out of here. There were gooseberry bushes and Rhubarb. Not much fruit to be had during the war time. We had plenty of prunes and custard and gooseberry or rhubarb pies. Plus English seasonal fruit mostly apples (russets). I remember seeing my first banana after the war and not knowing what it was.
When dad came home he would barter with traders taking newspaper and a load of mint from the garden to the butcher to get a few pence off the meat, (newspaper was used as wrapping paper at that time).
We also had a well in the garden and if the water was cut off for some reason, dad would lower a bucket on a string and we would have lovely clear water.
He used to shop for meat in the market but wouldn't take a shopping bag instead he took a hessian sack. One day mum and I were wondering why he was so late coming home. When he finally got home, mum asked why he was so late; he laughingly told her he had been in clink. A policeman had stopped him to ask what was in the sack. Dad showed him the meat and told him he had bought it in the market but until they found out he had not stolen it they locked him in the cell. Also because of rationing there was

an illegal black market racket going on and they probably thought he had done a deal on the black market. I think he probably had but whoever sold it to him wouldn't admit it as they also would get locked up. We laughed about it for ages.

Since my birth all the places I knew before 1964 have been demolished.
When I left School at 15 years I moved from job to job, being paid very low wages. My wages started at £1 per week for 40 hours.
They are still in my mind's eye, our House on Pickering Road, the church I was christened at, St Michaels and All Angels, Neepsend, Hillfoot County School, both grandparents' houses on Wallace Rd and Reginald St. The shops were we did our shopping on Meadow St. All the picture houses have now gone e.g. Oxford, Unity, Walkley Palladium, and many more. The Methodist chapel and St Michaels prefab, my places of work in Sheffield Joseph Rodgers and sons, Pond Hill. Samuels Jewellers, High St, Cantors dress Shop, Leopold St, Baldwin Drapers, Meadow St.
All I have of these are my memories.

My last job was driving a 40 mile radius of Sheffield for" Irving White LTD", delivering engineers tools.
I met my future husband whilst delivering tools to Davy McKee where he worked.
We married in 1964 at Holy Trinity Church, Nursery St and I left Parkwood springs and went to live in Stannington.
My Mother died on Parkwood Springs in 1963 at 51 years old.
Father remained on Parkwood Springs.
He remarried in 1966 and moved in with his new Wife Evelyn and they stayed for a while longer on Parkwood, Then in about 1971 they moved to Walkley.

Later in 2004 we took our Grandchildren to the New Adventure Playground that had been built by the side of the ski village on Parkwood Springs.
I thought it was wonderful for the children enjoying playing on Parkwood Springs again; it brought back so many memories for me.
It was such a shame that in a few years time it would be a burnt out shell along with the ski slope.

Dads greenhouse.

Dolls House made by Mr Torry
from an old tea chest.

Above left our house notice the window is boarded up after the bomb blast and right mum, dad and me 1942.

Above left dad and Uncle Lewis on leave 1942 and right Barbara with the chickens.

Entertainment

People made their own entertainment.

The Parkwood Hotel and The Douglas Inn, locally known as the top house were very popular where Men took their Wives. *(No Women went in pubs alone in the 1940/50s)*
There were quit a few landlord changes. Thomas Webster was the landlord at the Douglas Inn during 1948, at some point The Laws, then Nelson and Muriel in the 1960s, Nelson played the piano at the weekends and someone would do a turn singing.

An old chap called Tommy who frequented the pub, told about his experiences after volunteering for service in the 1914-18 war facing terrible conditions in the trenches. He was wounded and lost part of his left arm later being discharged.

There were fishing clubs, trips were organised to the seaside, Cleethorpes or Skegness and a charabanc (Coach) was booked to take us all there. These were wonderful for all the families.

A Day Fishing

It was one of those sunny days when the charabanc took us to the tidal river Trent.
All the men set up on the bank side with their fishing baskets and rods while all us children ran off in the fields all around us, we climbed trees and looked over the hedge. In the next field we saw lots of what we thought were toadstools, they were as big as saucers so over the hedge and into the field we jumped. What a good time we had skimming them into the river and watching them float.
Meantime my dad sat on the bank saw all these mushrooms floating past him and wondered where they were coming from. He left his fishing tackle to investigate. When he saw all the mushrooms in the field he forgot about fishing and started to collect them. He also forgot that the river was tidal and the other fishermen watched as not only mushrooms were floating down river so was my dad's fishing tackle. What a laugh we all had, I don't know if dad ever got his fishing tackle back but I know he came home with a sack full of mushrooms that he shared with all the neighbours.
Of course the coach had to stop at a pub half way home and all the children got crisps and pop a real treat.
Then all the men needed a toilet stop, they lined up in a field with their backs to us, all the Women laughing at them. We sang all the old songs until we got home.

Fishing club, Parkwood Hotel.

During the bad winter of 1947 the snow came thick and fast. No salting then.
All the Children and Dads loved it. We sledged from the top of Vale Road and continued onto Douglas Rd until we came to the Arch were the snow stopped

One or two large Street Bonfires were held to celebrate the end of the War,
After that we shared bonfires on November 5th.

We all went to the many cinemas, swimming pools and public parks in Sheffield.
The swimming baths had slipper baths for people without bathrooms.

Mr George Hitchens as Father Christmas in Douglas Inn.
Mrs Rutherford centre.

Parkwood Springs Methodist Chapel

The Methodist Chapel got bombed at the bottom of Pickering Rd.
Provision was made available in a building on Douglas Terrace for Services.
Lots of children went to Sunday school there.

Every year a may queen was chosen for the May Day Festival and sermons were held.
(Sermons was the religious ceremony for the crowning of the may queen.)
On Whit Monday a May Day a festival was held in Hillsborough Park and we all walked in procession with banners held high, from the top of Parkwood Springs to Hillsborough Park.
The children all had new clothes and shoes for Whit Sunday. We would walk all the way there and back in our new shoes and got many a blister.
Hillsborough Park was set out with a raised square stage in the centre of the large grassed area and roped off for each congregation. Thousands of people came from all over the district. Hymns were sung.
All the May Queens sat up on the stage. Lots of other organisations would be there, The Boys Brigade, Scouts and Guides from every congregation.

Then on Tuesday Games were played on the recreation ground on Parkwood Springs. Later a New Methodist Chapel was built at the bottom of Pickering Rd, where it had been originally.

Left: Douglas Rd May Queens Walk around Parkwood Springs 1960`s
Right: Maureen Clixby, Sermons 1947

Sermons at Parkwood Springs Chapel, Douglas Terrace 1947.

Back row L to R Barbara Eadon, Girl unknown,
Mid row L to R Maureen Clixby, Enid Bingham "May Queen", Joan Pinder
Sitting front L to R Boy Unknown, Rosie Pinder, Brenda Hinchcliffe

Sermons 1947 with the Children of Parkwood Springs.

Above 1941 wreckage of Parkwood Springs Chapel at the bottom of Pickering Rd
Below 1950s the rebuilt Chapel.

After the war a new Chapel was built where it had stood before the war at the bottom of Pickering Rd.

The Chapel was also used as a polling station.
During the 1964 general election Mr George Darling stood as Labour party candidate for Sheffield Hillsborough ward. The turnout for Parkwood Springs was 100%.
George Darling won the seat with a massive majority.

St Michael and all Angels Church, Burton Rd, Neepsend, Sheffield

Artist impression by B. Warsop

1867. The first place of worship in Neepsend was built on a triangular piece of land between Ball St North and Burton Rd, was St Michaels and all Angels church at a cost of around £4500.
It was a Beautiful Church more richly decorated than neighbouring Churches.

Interior St Michaels and All Angels Neepsend.
Picture" Historic England"

20

It became a thriving place of worship and had lots of activities for the congregation of all age's boys, girls, men and women.
The curate's house/vicarage was on the corner of Harvest Lane and Platt St.

In 1873 the church vicarage was converted into a parochial institution and club room.
By 1921 the parish room became a gymnasium and play centre.
A vicarage was then purchased on Vale Rd, Parkwood Springs, by subscriptions vested in trustees.

It was involved with Neepsend National School.ie Neepsend Church of England School, Boyland St. Neepsend.
This had been transferred from Pitsmoor on the formation of St Michael's parish.
According to parish magazine records of 1921, (Sheffield City archives.)
St Michaels had a debating society. Meetings that took place in the church or Institute during March to December of that year were as follows.
Choir Practice,
Mother union Meeting,
Junior Communicants Guilds,
St Michaels Guild,
Parochial Church Guild.
Band of Hope,
Boy's Brigade,
Girl Guides.
As well as Church services there was Sunday school,
Bazaars, to fund the gym, jumble sales.
Football was for Boys Of all ages. 14 to 140
Rambles and Picnics.
Games and Billiards room, which could provide refreshments.
There was also the Operatic Society.

December 1921 a Bazaar raised £280 for the institute.
This was an enormous amount of money for 1921.

"St Michaels and all Angels" closed down during the war in 1942 as the congregation dwindled and was demolished in 1959.

Boar War Hero
Sergeant James Firth, 193 Douglas Rd, Parkwood Springs, wins the VC.
1874-1921 James Firth of Swellwell, Durham.
1st battalion of the Duke of Wellingtons Regiment won the Victoria Cross during the Boar war for two acts of bravery. On the 24th February 1900 at Plewmans farm near Arundel, Cape Colony, South Africa. Sergeant Firth picked up and carried to cover a lance corporal who was lying wounded and exposed to heavy fire. Later when the enemy advanced within a short distance of the firing line, Sergeant Firth rescued a second Lieutenant who was dangerously wounded and carried him over the crest of a ridge to safety. He himself was shot through the nose and eye while doing so.

James Firth was presented with the Victoria Cross by King Edward V11 on Thursday 25th July 1901 for his bravery.

The Boar War hero died on 29-05-1921 aged 47years and a full military service was held at St Michaels and all Angels Church, Neepsend.
The Service was conducted by the Rev HH Everson (vicar) and Rev CF Warby.
James was thought to have lived on Wallace Rd and after leaving the army became foreman in a local steelworks. His wife Mary is shown as living at 193 Douglas Rd, Parkwood Springs Sheffield.
Source: Victoria Cross and Chris Hobbs web site.

St Michaels and All Angels Operatic Society 1930`s
Top, Mikado. Bottom, Merry England.

Count of Como.

St Michaels and all Angels Boys Clubs circa 1918/20

Boys Brigade Back row 2nd left Alf Eadon 3rd Left Edward Eadon

Football Club, Sat left Edward Eadon sat right Alf Eadon

St Michaels Scouts

The Lady Chapel, St Michaels and All Angels

A prefabricated building was built in the Vicarage Grounds on Vale Rd to accommodate the Church of England Congregation. 1940`s-1950`s

The new "St Michaels and All Angels" prefabricated church on Vale Rd was then used for Sunday church services and as a community hall for other activities as had St Michaels church in the past.
There was the Mothers Union, Film Shows, and Socials. Etc.
We went carolling with the church all around Parkwood Springs and held lanterns and went in the pubs with collecting tins.

During the 1950's the youth club started meeting on Mondays.
We played games, table tennis, learned to ballroom dance, had trips to the seaside and went walks in the country.
Pantomimes were organised by the church committee and held at Rutland Hall, and Holy Trinity Church Hall.
During the 1950`s St Michaels Church joined with Holy Trinity on Nursery Street. There was a large congregation and a wonderful choir. Regular Saturday socials, badminton club, scouts and guides.
We walked all the way from the top of Parkwood Springs to Nursery St and back.

St Michaels Youth club trip to Cleethorpes.

Back row left to Right: Terry Higgins, Trevor Barnes, Terry Mitchell, and Raymond Swift.
Front Row left to right: Keith Woodhead, Ralph Mitchell, Jean White, Melna Parkin, Barbara Eadon, Maureen Clixby and Michael Walker.

Above: St Michaels Mothers Union Trips.

Cinderella Pantomime

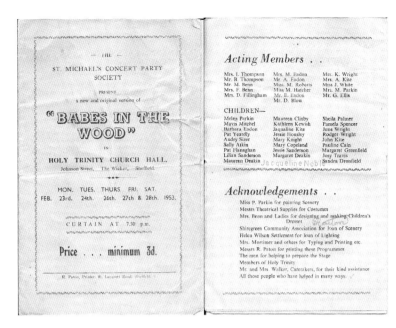

- THE -

ST. MICHAEL'S CONCERT PARTY SOCIETY

PRESENT

a new and original version of

"BABES IN THE WOOD"

IN

HOLY TRINITY CHURCH HALL,

Johnson Street, The Wicker, Sheffield.

MON. TUES. THURS. FRI. SAT.
FEB. 23rd. 24th. 26th. 27th & 28th. 1953.

CURTAIN AT 7.30 p.m.

Price . . . minimum 3d.

R. Paton, Printer, 46, Langsett Road, Sheffield.

Acting Members . .

Mrs. I. Thompson	Mrs. M. Eadon	Mrs. K. Wright
Mr. B. Thompson	Mr. A. Eadon	Mrs. A. Kite
Mr. M. Benn	Miss. M. Roberts	Miss J. White
Mrs. F. Benn	Miss M. Hatcher	Mrs. M. Parkin
Mrs. D. Fillingham	Mr. E. Eadon	Mr. G. Ellis
	Mr. D. Blow	

CHILDREN—

Melea Parkin	Maureen Clixby	Sheila Palmer
Mavis Mitchel	Kathleen Kewish	Pamela Spencer
Barbara Eadon	Jaqualine Kite	June Wright
Pat Yeardly	Jessie Housley	Rodger Wright
Audry Sizer	Mary Knight	John Kite
Sally Atkin	Mary Copeland	Pauline Cain
Pat Flanaghan	Jessie Sanderson	Margaret Greenfield
Lilian Sanderson	Margaret Deakin	Josy Travis
Maureen Deakin		Sandra Dronfield

Acknowledgements . .

Miss P. Parkin for painting Scenery
Messrs Theatrical Supplies for Costumes
Mrs. Benn and Ladies for designing and making Children's Dresses
Shiregreen Community Association for loan of Scenery
Helen Wilson Settlement for loan of Lighting
Mrs. Mortimer and others for Typing and Printing etc.
Messrs R. Paton for printing these Programmes
The men for helping to prepare the Stage
Members of Holy Trinity
Mr. and Mrs. Walker, Caretakers, for their kind assistance
All those people who have helped in many ways.

1953 Programme

All the Cast of Babes in the Wood

Babes in the Wood

Back row, L to R Alf Eadon, George Ellis, Bernard Thompson, and Donald Blow.
Kneeling, L to R Maurice Benn, Edward Eadon.

Below back row L to R, Maureen Deakin, Kathleen Kewish, Kath Wright, Jean White, Barbara Eadon, and Maureen Clixby.
Front row L to R, Mrs Kite, Mrs Eadon, Mrs Parkin, Mrs Benn, Mrs Fillingham, and Mrs Thompson.

War Time 1939-45

Some of the men on Parkwood Springs were called upon to serve their Country, others worked in reserved occupations e.g.: railway or steel.
Alfred Eadon, Lewis Page and Stanley Rooker were a few of Parkwooders who among many were called up.
Alfred Eadon was in the Royal Army Catering Corp`s
Lewis Page was in the Royal Navy and served on HMS Viceroy
Stanley Rooker was in the Royal Navy and served on HMS Lapwing.

At the top of Parkwood Springs there was an "Anti Aircraft Gun Emplacement" with Ack-Ack guns a Barrage Balloon and Rocket guns. The rocket guns that could be manned by women fired in all directions to detract the Germans.
The base of which can still be seen today.

It was a terrible time for everyone; several people were killed when a bomb dropped at the corner of Pickering Rd and Wallace Rd, also destroying the Methodist chapel.
Another bomb dropped onto a gas tank causing a fire but fortunately no explosion. Many houses suffered bomb damage some with large holes in the roof so people had to live with friends or relatives until repairs could be done.
Mr Sands a railway driver had just left the engine sheds when the sirens went and he was helping children into the shelter when the explosion from a bomb threw him into the shelter killing him, it was horrific.

The ridiculous thing was that some children were evacuated to Sheffield from London, and a few came to live on Parkwood.
Just after the blitz Bill Ronksley who lived at Stannington had to walk to work at the engine sheds on Parkwood Springs because all the transport had stopped due to the destruction in Sheffield City centre. When he got to Hillfoot Bridge, there were many women carrying cases walking with about fifty children. Bill asked them where they were going and if he could help. They told him they were walking to the railway station, they were evacuees from London and if the bombs are dropping here they may as well go home. Bill helped them carry their cases to the station.

During the Second World War a quarter of the houses on Parkwood Springs were destroyed by bombing. The houses were not rebuilt and the sites were either left partly derelict or occupied with industrial users. There were promises of redevelopment but by 1970s people were being re-housed as far away Mosborough.

Anecdotes and Embellishments
Memories told at our reunions.

Many characters lived on Parkwood, Charlie Watson who ran the corner shop on Wallace Rd being one such, he used to get us kids to take back the wrappers off chocolate wagon wheel biscuits, we never knew why until one day we watched him through the window. He gathered all the crumbs out of the bag and ate them.

My father Alf Eadon was also a character. We had a very large garden so after the war he became a keen gardener. Anything he could get hold of to make compost was the norm. Working at the brewery after the hops had been used they had to be got rid of, so my dad asked if they could be delivered to our house and a lorry load was dropped onto the pavement outside our house. Dad had to shovel them over our six foot wall at the bottom of our very long garden. It smelled like a brewery for ages, I think we all got drunk on the smell alone whatever our neighbours thought is anyone's guess. He never did get around to using them all.

He also asked the chimney sweep to dump the soot from our chimney onto the garden. This soot and Trevor Barnes got me into terrible trouble with my mum. Trevor goaded me into jumping into the soot. Why ever I listened to him I will never know. Was I a good sport or a fool? Anyway I jumped and clouds of soot covered me from head to toe and Trevor fell about laughing. When I ran home, I can't tell you what my mum thought about Trevor Barnes. If you have ever tried to wash off soot you will know that it floats. Remember we had no bathroom and mum put me straight into the sink clothes and all and the soot floated all around us. It took ages for mum to clean it all away.

From that day on I was told to stay away from Trevor Barnes.

Decorating the walls during wartime brought out creative ideas, we painted the walls with distemper and then for effect stippled them with a potato cut in half or a bit of old rag dipped in different colours and dabbed all over the wall. It took ages but looked good when finished. We could bring out a new fashion today with this.

Washing days on Parkwood could be very frustrating as clothes hung out to dry would get smuts of black soot from the steam trains and went grey with all the smoke from the industrial furnaces in Sheffield.

We never noticed the pollution until we went on holiday when on the way home you could see a pall of smoke hung over Sheffield like a fog and smell it after breathing the fresh air at the sea side.

Another annoying thing when we got televisions was the ghosting across the picture when the gas tanks were high. We all just accepted it and laugh about it now.

When living in a terraced house you had to share the back yard with neighbours so sometimes there was conflict. In that space there were rows of outside toilets and coal bunkers. If two people had dogs that the others were fed up with all hell could break loose?

In the 1950s a joke shop opened in town and someone bought a false poo to have a joke with the dog owners in the yard, placing it on one of the dog owner's step and waiting for the action to take place. When the woman came out and saw this she marched to the other dog owner and accused her dog of the offence, this started a big row both women shouting at one another. After a while the joker nonchalantly walked over and picked the false poo up and put it in his pocket to the astonishment of the women. The shouting then turned to laughter.

1946 Dangerous times dangerous games.

After the war Roger Simcox who lived on Parkwood Rd recalls roaming around the hillside with friends searching through the rubble where the Ack-Ack guns had been, and finding bullets which they took to have some fun with. The railway footbridge at that time was made of wood and they lit a fire underneath it and threw the bullets onto the fire then ran as fast as they could to watch what happened.

It's a wonder they were not killed as the bullets shot out in all directions and the bangs nearly deafened them. Luckily no one was hurt and it didn't set fire to the bridge. Sometimes children took bullets they had found to school and one day a child took into school a hand grenade and all the children had to be evacuated until it was dealt with. Goodness knows how he acquired that.

On the recreation ground was a workman's hut, Ray Swift and Roy Heywood from Mount Rd felt very cold one day and one of them had found a lighter so they decided to light a fire under the bench in this hut to get warm, the fire got out of hand and they had to get out fast. The hut burned down and they both blamed one another for it.

Ray laughingly told us about the returned empty bottle theft. Bottles had a deposit on them and when returned to the shop you got your money back. Mr Tingle at the beer off on Mount Rd used to store these returned bottles in a crate outside at the back of the shop. The children found them took them and kept returning them, until Mr Tingle cottoned onto their little game.

Bull roaring, Drain pipes were made of cast iron and boys put rolled up news paper into the bottom of the drain pipe and set it alight, the air would suck it up to the top roaring as it went.

Bonfire nights were the best time for boys to get up to mischief. We all shared bonfires with neighbours, sitting on old chairs or settees that had been brought to burn later. Enjoying jacket potatoes, toffee apples, bonfire toffee, chestnuts' found in the woods. Then during the 1950s fireworks became available, bangers, jumping jacks, Catherine wheels, sparklers. The bangers were very loud. Boys used to put the jumping jacks under peoples chairs to make them jump. One time a jumping jack jumped under a settee which an old lady was sat on and it started to smoulder, she had to be helped off quickly and the settee put on the fire.
Some boys found an empty oil drum behind some garages and decided to tie a few bangers together light them and drop them in the drum and run. The bang nearly deafened them and they thought they had blown up the garages. Luckily they hadn't.

Illnesses 1940s

Some people were in the "St John's Ambulance Association," and gave first aid.
To visit a Doctor you had to pay. Because of this a few Quack Doctors existed to help people out. *Quack Doctor An unqualified practitioner.*
Illnesses were rife. This was before the NHS.
There were all the usual Childhood Illnesses, Mumps. Measles, Chicken pox, Whooping Cough and more.
A few terrible ones were Rickets, Tuberculosis, Polio, Scabies, Bronchitis, Tonsillitis, and Diphtheria.
Impetigo was a very contagious runny spot and usually on the face, Treated with deep "Purple crystal violet."
So everyone knew who had it. Lots of us went to school painted with this purple colour.
After suffering with polio Children had to wear irons on their legs for support.

Without antibiotics even Tonsillitis would put a child in bed for a week with a fever.

Hillfoot County School

Artist's impression Of Hillfoot School, Sandbed Road and photo of boys school gate 2015

Between Sandbed Road and Waterford Rd, Neepsend School opened 1891 by the side of the river Don.
The main Building had three separate schools each with its own head teacher and staff.
The School was the first free School in Sheffield and provided accommodation for 720 pupils between 5 and 10 years.
In 1899 the school reorganised into a mixed senior, junior and infants, with 767 pupils.

(Free school meaning free education)
In 1903 it became Neepsend Council School
In 1926 the Hillfoot Council School,
In 1944 it became Hillfoot County School
In 1958 Hillfoot Junior Mixed and Infants School.

It was an all age School until 1958. After that senior children were transferred to Chaucer Secondary School. It was closed on the 25th July 1975 due to the almost complete disappearance of the area's population.

Most of the children of Parkwood Springs attended Hillfoot County School.
Others went to Woodside School.

We called it Skoyal. We all spoke broad Yorkshire.

The route to Hillfoot School from the top of Pickering Rd was down the narrow cobble stoned Genel with a hand rail in the centre, which led to the Station Steps, at the top of Wallace Rd over the Railway Bridge to Parkwood Rd and Hoyland Rd and onto Sandbed Rd by the side of the River Don.
Quite a trek all up and down the steep hill and very icy during the winter, but we loved to slide down it.

On the way to School we did acrobats on the railings, hop scotch on the pavement, and loved to watch out for the trains going under the Railway Bridge, it would be wonderful if we saw the Flying Scotsman.

There was also a fairy castle carved into the rock on the other side of the railway line and some of us were goaded to cross the line to see this.

This was a very dangerous thing to do.
Time didn't mean a thing to us.
It must have taken us ages to get to School.
Two boys Don Alexander and Alan Cottingham on their way to school from Parkwood Road which should have taken 15 minutes to get to school took them over half an hour.
The boys had to look among the bombed out ruins for ¬Deead -bodies;
Ears had to be pressed against the tramway poles to catch the hum of a distant tram.
The crimped steel bottle tops from the vinegar factory had to be skimmed across the Rd.
The steel bars at Toledo's wire rod mill had to be watched, revolving at high speed, with the billets getting smaller and longer all very hypnotic.

Their Idyllic progress was brutally halted one day when they were looking over Hillfoot Bridge at the River Don in full flow after heavy rain.
A gang of school bullies got hold of them punching Don in the nose, " ah gorrim reight on nooase" he said, worse they then held them both by the ankles over the river. "Don't worry Donald" said Allan, their faces next to one another upside down. "They daren`t drop us". This was just an everyday occurrence of the time in Neepsend.

All this dawdling made them late for School one day, their punishment was the cane.
Teachers were very fond of the cane, some more than others.
They would be caned in front of the whole class of 40+ as an example to others, or would be sent to the head teacher for six of the best.
They were caned on the palms of their hands and would come back in class with both hands red and swollen,
Boys were caned on a regular basis for messing about in the class.
How cruel was that.
It never made any difference it only served to release the teacher's frustration at not being able to control the class.
Lots of bullying took place among the children, but what would you expect when the teachers acted that way.
We were taught the three Rs. and geography.
The only history I remember was about royalty.
It meant nothing to very poor children.
For domestic science we were given tokens to go on the bus to Wisewood School and for games we were transported by coach to the school field on Myers Grove Lane, Stannington.
Other lessons were hygiene (cleanliness) and sewing for girls and woodwork and metalwork for boys.
Physical exercise was very important and was done on a regular basis in the school yard.

After the war," Sheffield City Council" arranged for a few children from each school in Sheffield to hear The Halle Orchestra Play classical music at the City Hall.
Mr Stones our music teacher arranged for us to go if we wanted to.
Coaches were laid on for us to get there.
When we got to the City Hall there were loads of coaches full of children all pouring out of the coaches and into the city hall to hear classical music. It was magic.
The City Hall was packed with children and not a sound was heard from them when the Orchestra was playing.
Sir John Barbirolli was the conductor.

Hillfoot County School 1947 and 1948

Below 1953

34

Boys Brigade back row second from right Donald Alexander
Courtesy Donald Alexander

Our route to School down the station steps and over the railway bridge as it is today
2015

Neepsend School 1902 / later becoming (Hillfoot County School)

Children made banners for Peace after the Boar War when 96% of solders from Hillsborough Barracks were killed leaving the Women alone to bring up their families.

Hillfoot School fainting episode

Around about 1953 during morning assembly a child fainted who was stood at the front of me and had to be helped out, the next minute two more children fainted. It was very disturbing for the rest of the children.
It became a phenomenon episode of great proportions after that.
All morning children were fainting and were laid out on the benches in the open air shed in the school yard. Ambulances had to be sent for. They were all taken to the Royal Infirmary hospital. They all came back to school the next day. The doctors at the hospital found nothing wrong with them.

George Orwell on Parkwood Springs

George Orwell lodged with Mr and Mrs Searle at 154, Wallace Road, Parkwood Springs when staying in Sheffield to research his book "The Road to Wigan Pier".
His publisher Victor Gollancz wanted him to research the unemployment of the north of England
All Orwell's doubts about it vanished when his publisher paid him £500 for the book, the equivalent of two years pay.

Kate Searle, who was 29 at the time, was a committed socialist and secretary to the women's section of the Lansdowne Labour Party.
She said of Orwell in an article in the Sheffield Telegraph dated February 2 1990

"He was a very jolly fellow, very intelligent - he`d been educated at Eton. He used to go out with my husband to lots of socialist meetings in town. He wanted to see how the other half lived. He used to say to us I cannot understand you people, you are so strong willed and you know about life yet you don`t stand up to the upper classes.
I think he had good intentions in trying to write about the working class but as I said to him you have to live with us for more than one week to find out what it's all about. "

Bernard Crick "George Orwell - A Life". Recounts that he was shown around Sheffield by a partially crippled unemployed communist activist called William Brown. It was through Brown that Orwell lodged with the Searle`s in Wallace Rd. He was charged six shillings a week for his board and lodgings.
He visited many meetings, factories and houses. He left the Searle`s after just 3 days and went to stay with his sister and brother in law in Leeds.

Orwell said on leaving Sheffield I was quite sorry to leave the Searle's. I have seldom met people with more natural decency. They were kind to me as anyone could possibly be, and hope that they liked me.
Of course I got their whole life history from them by degrees.
Searle is 33 and was an only child. When a youth he joined the Army Ordnance Corps and was with the army in Palestine and Egypt and wishes he was back there. Since then he has only had short lived jobs, as store keeper and check- weigh man at various works, also railway porter. Searle married his wife when he was on the dole against her father's

wishes.

When they married they couldn`t get a house and lived in one room, here they had two children and one died. They told me they had only one bed and had to lay the child out in a perambulator.

Finally after frightful difficulty "because he was on the dole" they managed to get the house on Wallace Rd, the rent was 8s .6d. Kate earned 9s a week from her charring. Exactly what deduction is made for this from Searle's dole I don`t know, but their total income is 32s. 6d.

Kate and George Searle were very proud people and would only ask Orwell to pay 6s for full board and lodgings from Monday night to Thursday morning. They keep the house very clean and decent. The garden was small and they can`t do much with it as it has chimneys at one side and gas works at the other, with poor soil. Mrs Searle's grasp of the economic situation was surprising her abstract ideas- quite unlike most working-class women. She thought the people who employed her were kind and is not resentful against them. In domestic service she calculated the price of the food she served on the table, for 5 persons for one meal it came to 6s. 3d, this is as much as the PACs. (Public assistance committee) allows her for her child for two weeks.

In order to qualify for dole a worker had to pass a means test The Public Assistance Committee PACs put the worker`s finances through a vigorous investigation before they could qualify for benefit.. Officials went into every detail of a family's income and savings. The intrusiveness of the means test and the insensitive manner of the officials who carried it out frustrated and offended the workers. (Taken from the National Archives website)

William Brown was the man who showed Orwell around Sheffield and from morning until night he was rushed from place to place largely on foot to see public buildings, slums and housing estates etc. Orwell thought Brown was too conscious of his Communist convictions and tiresome to be with, being quite a disgruntled person.

Brown thought Orwell was a bourgeois and remarked on Orwell's public school twang, but was very generous and would go out of his way to spare Orwell the expense of meals. "Source Chris Hobbs website"

1940 to 1960: Games

Childhood on Parkwood Springs was wonderful.

All Parkwood Springs was our playground. Games were played across the road as there were no cars. We were sent out to play and didn't go home until we were hungry. Children could go into anyone's garden or house on Parkwood and be safe and welcome.

Gas lamps had a cross bar for the lamplighter to lean his ladder on to light the gas. String was tied to the cross bar we would get a good swing on that.

We played for hours on the wood sliding down the grass on cardboard or in a tin bath, in winter we would be on our sledges in the snow having great fun.

Then there was the rec (recreation ground), which had swings and a roundabout and lots of grass and space. There were toilets, and a water fount. (See photo)

All the girls loved it when in summer the tarmac melted and bubbled up through the cobble stones, we would sit and poke it out and role it into balls and throw it at one another, and got very dirty. We were in terrible trouble for doing this as it would not come off your clothes in the wash.

All the children on Parkwood got up to mischief especially when it went dark.
We knocked at doors and ran away, or tied two door knobs together and then hide to see the commotion when two people tried to open their door, or tied someone's door knob to a bin lid so that when the door was opened the bin lid came flying off with a loud bang.
One day the children went a bit too far by tying the string to the handles of the bin so that it fell over and the contents spilled over into the yard. A neighbour caught them; they had never heard such language.
Also one of the houses had a hook over the kitchen window and the children decided to have fun with it by tying a few buttons onto a piece of fine string, hanging them onto the hook so they reached the window then with the other end leading to the passage they hid and pulled the string so that the buttons tapped on the window.
This could go on for ages as the person didn't know who or what was tapping on their window.

Other games were Mabs (Marbles) five stones, rounder's, skipping with a bull rope across the road, tiggy of the ground, tiggy bob down, statues, Mr Wolf, Farmers in the den, Kiss catch, kick can, pickup sticks, hop scotch, and sometimes the boys let the girls join in with Cricket. All in all we had lots of fun.

We also played in the Hallamshire Steel Billet Storage yard- risking life and limb of something toppling over as we climbed on the stacked up billets or cutting ourselves on the sharp ends. Odd occasions we would play on the `bombed buildings` A remnant of the blitz, and poke around, to see what if anything, we could find, never did though.

The boys would make Winter Warmers out of clay from the quarry.
The clay was formed into a box with two holes in the side and baked in the oven until hard. Then they got an oily wap and put this in the winter warmer and lit it, and swung it round sometimes. (An oily wap was a dirty piece of rag full of oil from the factory).
Roger Simcox of Parkwood Road made one for his son in the 1960`s and brought it to our reunion. He tells of some rough lads who would gang up on weaker boys to bully them. One day they took a boy to the quarry and made him eat the clay.

Parkwood springs water fount and toilet block Courtesy Peter Addison.

Toilet block Parkwood rec

38

A Tribute to George Ellis

George Lived at the top of Pickering Rd.
I remember George as a very prominent member of St Michael and all Angels' church,
He worked tirelessly along with our Vicar Mr Naylor running the youth club in the 1950`s
taking us walking, trips to the Sea Side, teaching us ballroom dancing, table tennis,
billiards, organising film shows, in the Church Hall, Laurel and Hardy, Charlie Chaplin,
and other silent films all favourites with the children of Parkwood Springs and Neepsend.
The church hall was full with children, entertaining them at little expense.

Then in 1952/53 he was joint Director with Bernard Thomson, Douglas Rd, of two
Pantomimes, The first being "Cinderella" and the following year "Babes in the Wood".
They were very popular with lots of people; all the members of the church plus the wider
Community became involved.
We became Actors, Singers, and Dancers etc.
We all had our part to play in the organisation of such a wonderful thing.
There were rehearsals.
A Dance teacher was arranged to teach tap dancing to the girls.
Costumes had to be made by the ladies of the church. Scenery had to be painted.
Lighting to do and Photographs to be taken.
The entire congregation took part; Mums, Dads and Children.
This took up lots of our time, so goodness knows how much time George spared for all of
us. He was such a fun person; there wasn't anything that was too much trouble for him.
The Pantomimes were a great success with the public filling "Rutland Hall" on Rutland
Rd and Holy Trinity, Church Hall. Nursery St, Wicker.

When it was Queen Elizabeth's Coronation he built a Television in his cellar and invited a
few people to watch the event.
I remember going and seeing the wires all around the cellar and this small blue screen
nothing like you would imagine a TV to be like.
We thought it was magic even though we could hardly make out the picture.
What an achievement.
He mended lots of Televisions for the people of Parkwood.
I lost touch with George years ago. But I will remember him with affection for all he did
for Parkwood Springs making it a magic place to live and be part of.

Left to right, George Ellis, Keith Woodhead, Barbara Eadon, Maureen Clixby, Trevor
Barnes, Jean White, Colin White, Maureen Deakin, Mary Eadon.

A Gale hit Sheffield on February 16th 1962

The 96 miles per hour Gale did a lot of damage on Parkwood Springs being on a hill it lifted the roof completely off the house at the top of Pickering Rd and dropped it whole by the side of the house. It blew Mrs Barnes television aerial sideways and smashed through their window and I went to help put a sheet up but we were battling with the wind and sheet for ages. Roof slates and bricks were flying all over the place. On Mount Rd a complete gable end was destroyed. The next morning it looked like the wartime again. Brick's glass slates everywhere.

Slum Clearances

Then the call came for Slum clearance from "Sheffield City Council"
The Secretary of State for the Environment in exercise of his powers under the housing act of 1953 declared some land to be cleared.
Houses not being fit for habitation will have to be demolished. We were shocked because these were our homes.
We all knew then that we were going to have to leave Parkwood and some people started to leave before it became compulsory.
Most of us were in private rented accommodation, either from the Railway or Private landlords.

In 1973 Parkwood Springs was issued with a compulsory purchase order.
This became very distressing for the remaining people.
Some of the houses became dangerous for children playing as they used to.
It became difficult to live there as before, so again George Ellis along with my father, Alfred Eadon, Church and Chapel and many others from the wider community became involved trying to make things better. Until the inevitable came, and there was nothing else to do but move out.
People were being moved into houses all over Sheffield destroying the wonderful community that had existed there for a 100 years.
A Parkwood Springs, "Community Action Group" was set up.
The Community action group got in touch with 'Sheffield City Council". A Community House was provided at 52 Mount Rd. Parkwood Springs for the benefit of the remaining residents.

A leaflet was produced called.
  "Parkwood Echo"
The Voice of Parkwood Springs
George Ellis was the Chairman.

There were 14 representatives on the action committee plus 5 co-opted representatives consisting of people from, Christ Church Pitsmoor, the Methodist Chapel, and Headmaster from Hillfoot School, A Social Worker, and a Student.
Once again the cry went out to Sheffield City Council to be more sympathetic to Parkwood Springs Needs.
But we were always the forgotten village.

It's now 2016 and it's still the Forgotten Village.

Past residents contributions of stories

Peter Addison
110, Pickering Road

Mr and Mrs Addison had eight children - One child Brian died aged seventeen years. Just before the last one was born Mr Addison aged 50 years passed away leaving Mum to bring up the seven children alone. This was very hard for her but she did her best.

Peter remembers the games he played with his brother, roaming around the rec and allotments and the river Don Waterside.

They made bows and arrows, having competitions to see how far the arrows would fly. The bows were made from tree branches and string and the arrows were made from willow herb or dried stalks of moon pennies; the metal tip was a piece of rusty metal cable wire they found near the old cable cars that used to carry coal to the power station tip (black Ash) from the gas works.
When playing with this one day his brother shot Peter in the wrist with the arrow.
Oh dear! Peter had to have poultices on for weeks after by the doctor, before it would heal.
The same brother put the kettle directly on the fire instead of the grid and Peter was sitting at the front of the fire in his pyjamas when the kettle fell over and he was scalded. He still remembers this and still has the scars on his ankle.

Peter has collected lots of history about Parkwood Springs and often helps people do their family tree.

Douglas Terrace. Photo courtesy of Peter Addison

Jean Addison nee Ward

We used to love it if a train passed under the bridge on way to School. We would wave to the train driver, and to the man in the signal box. Some of the lads used to throw stones at the signal box, and if he came out everyone would leg it.

In summer we'd spend hours on the "rec" as we called it. I used to go in some of the old allotments to pick flowers for my mam. There were sweet peas, roses, tiger lilies, and you could get moon pennies by the armful, as well as lupines' and bluebells.

A group of us kids off Douglas Terrace used an old allotment as a hangout we tried to cadge bits and bobs for it from home or anyone. We all pooled our money which bought some sausages and a tin of beans and the older lads made a fire and the food was cooked in an old saucepan and passed round, anyway someone said that the Gypsies were above the pigsties on the wood.
(The wood was any part of the hillside facing Douglas Rd)
After all agreeing on a visit to them, we`d got an old mushroom basket, then had a look in other empty allotments and filled it with flowers, mint, and I think rhubarb.
We made our way up the wood and when we got nearer, the eldest two which were lads told us to wait in case they chased us off.

We were called up and a Man thanked us for the things and told us to sit down on the grass.
Then he got out a violin and started playing for us,
We were all stunned I doubt any of us had seen a violin being played in the flesh,
I recall the caravans were round topped but can`t remember seeing any horses.
The Man was wearing tight knee length boots with trousers tucked inside,
(I had only ever seen trousers tucked in wellingtons) he also had on a dark waist coat.
We were all a bit gob smacked and pleased we`d visited them.

Some days we would watch men playing bowls at the bowling green, but we had to behave or the park keeper would throw us out.

I remember having a stick of rhubarb dipped in sugar, and buying monkey nuts from the fruit man that used to come round with his horse and cart.
They used to go on fishing trips with the Douglas pub, and when they arrived back they would throw pennies out of the charabanc window, and all us kids would scramble for the pennies.

We used to go to the "chippy" for a bag of chips and a pickled onion, and on Friday tea time I used to have to go to the back door of the chippie with a half a crown for two bob's worth of wet fish, and sixpence worth of potatoes, and my mam would cook fish for me dad, and make fish cakes for us. My dad would have fish and potatoes with oxo gravy (Yuk!)

The tradesmen used to come round, the lovely ice cream man in his little van (Mr Manfredi, an Italian), and he always asked "do you want red on it?" meaning raspberry sauce.
There was a man, who used to come on a push bike with a large basket calling Oatcakes and Pikelats.
Not forgetting the blind man who sold sandalwood soap and other things. My mam

always bought soap from him, and he was always trusting. He would tell you to help yourself to the change.

Also an Indian man came up in turban, but most people were scared of them, so we wouldn't answer the door.

Mr Hammond the fruit man came with his horse and cart and his sons and grandsons would be helping him sometimes. If his horse had mucked on the road, someone would come and shovel it up after he'd gone and put it on their flowers.

At weekends Bill North used to bring veg round, and we also had Bob the butcher in his little van.

A policeman used to come round with his push-bike every night. And one of us kids used to sit out of a ball game to watch out for him, because ball games were not allowed. It was no big deal, just a way of life.

Down the opposite side of Douglas Road was what we called "the wood", and at the top of the wood was a quarry, which was run by Gleeson's. There was another quarry at the bottom of Douglas Road ran by the brick yard, which is where my mum worked for many years, as did Mrs Knifeton who lived on Douglas Terrace.

Most of the people didn't have bathrooms, and the toilets were outside.

We would have squares of newspaper hung behind the door, and in winter we would put a candle inside a bottle and leave it stood next to the cistern, and hope that it would stop it from freezing.

The hot water bottle you took to bed wasn't rubber. It was an oven plate wrapped in a rag.

Our cooker was a black lead range which was an oven and an open fire and my mom used to cook everything in the oven, and boil the kettle on the fire. As I got older my mum had a two ring gas cooker with a grill underneath. I remember doing a big dish of potatoes and onions in gravy and boiling bacon bones for us to pick on (they call them spare ribs nowadays). I loved her seasoned Yorkshire Puddings with fried onions and thick gravy.

Our first washer was my mum with a barrel and a rubbing board, and a mangle that she kept on top of the cellar. Everyone washed on a Monday, and underwear was boiled in a saucepan or in a boiler.

Parkwood Springs to me always seemed a safe place to live. I loved my childhood, I didn't have much but then again I didn't starve.

I remember one really bad time though when my dad slipped a disc and was off work for nine months. I know we didn't have anything for Christmas and a kind neighbour knocked on our door with bags of food and presents and my great aunt gave my mom five pounds, which was a lot of money then, and my mom sat down and cried and said how good people were.

I think the worst thing I ever did as a kid was knock on people's doors and run away. My dad was strict and if I would have done any worse than that his belt would have come off. I had a taste of the belt a few times.

Sometimes my mum would take us train spotting near the mine, and we might take some potted meat sandwiches, and a bottle of lemonade, and if we were really lucky we would go to Riverlin to the paddling pool. It seemed miles away, and the water would be freezing but we didn't care, we loved it. We would spend hours in the water. It was like going to the seaside without the sand.

Having a bath by the coal fire was lovely, and all of us had to use the same water but when I think about, it must have been hard work for my mum boiling all those kettles of water, then afterwards taking the full bath full of water outside to empty it and pour it down the drain.

I remember when we had been to my uncle's piggery and my sister, Linda, had fallen in the pig muck up to her neck. It was fresh that morning and the smell nearly knocked you out. She cried all the way home because no-one would carry her. She had to have a bath outside because of the smell, and then my mum scrubbed the bath out with San Izal disinfectant. I didn't know what was the worse smell, the pig muck or the San Izal. Everyone on our street saved all their stale bread and vegetables for my uncle's pigs. He left two dustbins outside my grandmother's for people to fill. If he had been to the fruit market for fruit and vegetables for the pigs, he'd let you pick out good fruits to take home.

I've always been frightened of thunder storms and my mom hated them, and she would cover anything that was metal and even take her metal hair clips out, and cover the mirror. And if a storm started in the night my mom would awaken me and my sister Linda and make us sit at the top of the cellar with a blanket over our heads. If we had a storm in the daytime and my dad was at home, my dad would stand at the back door and shout "bring it down David". My mom would go barmy telling him to get in.

If we had a bad cough my mom and dad would put butter, vinegar and sugar in a saucer and put it in the oven to warm and then we would have to drink it (if they were lucky). I was pinned down and my nose held until I opened my mouth, then a large spoonful was poured down my throat. It was horrible.

I can remember in the winter I saw the bread man, the coal man and the milk man dragging their wares up Douglas Road on sledges when it was thick snow, as there were no gritting wagons for us. The only bus that went up there was a single Decker, just a few years before it was demolished.

When we had water shortages in hot summers. A small water tanker was at the end of Douglas Terrace and everyone would queue with their buckets, bowls and jugs.
A man used to come round to clean sewer grates. You were always told to keep away from fever grates.

There was nobody playing loud music, as everyone had respect for their neighbours. As I got in to my teens I got a liking for pop music I had a small transistor radio given to me, and I used to sit and listen to radio Caroline, and the top 40.
I had to buy batteries for it with my babysitting money.
In the summer we'd have top of the pops on and we'd dance in the back yard, and some older ones in the yard would say "them Beatles and Rolling Stones are like lasses. They need a bloody good hair cut" and anyone who sang on the top of the pops were rubbish in my dad's eyes.
And if we wore make up my dad would say "get that muck off your face" and in winter if you had a short skirt on my dad would say "cover them legs up, you'll catch your death of cold".

Jean`s Poem

Parkwood Springs to me was a happy place
There was plenty to do and lots of space
A walk to school was such a trek
But did we care, did we heck

Most of us lived two up two down
With no direct bus into town
With outside lavs and no soft loo role
Newspaper, to answer natures call

We had a recreation ground to do us proud
And a bowling green, which gathered a big crowd
With lots of allotments to grow your veg
Surrounded by walls and a leafy hedge

We played cricket, rounder's and tiggy too
We found lots of things that we all could do
From scrumping to bonfires and putting on a show
To carting and sledging and playing in the snow

The luxury of a car would be a treat
But most of our trips were by our own two feet
Winter in wellingtons, slapping our legs
And don't forget oven plate in our beds

Boiling hot summers, no water to drink
Reservoir dried up and fever grates stink
Not many of us had money to spare
But those that had, we all could share

It was a village, a hamlet, our own Shangri la
And many who left, wished they hadn't gone far
But looking at it now, it's a land fill tip
It's enough to make your language slip

Trevor Barnes
69 Pickering Rd

Born 18th June 1938, Delivered by the local midwife, Nurse Freeman, who lived in Wallace Road.

Father, Ernest, Silversmith at James Dixon's. Mother Nellie worked in the warehouse at James Dixon's.

GP was Dr Harding, an Irishman whose surgery was on Montgomery Terrace Road.

Next door neighbour at 71 was Mrs Hardy; Her Brother Vin Hardy had a fruit and veg business. He used to come round with his horse and cart.
Our milkman was Joe Lumby.
Just below us was Puttergill's paper shop at 65.
There were two other shops in Pickering Road, Briddon's lower down and Parrot's at the top.
The very top house in Pickering Road was Woodhead's. Mrs Woodhead did hairdressing in the front room. They were quite posh and had a phone. I didn't know of anybody else having one at that time.

I went to Hillfoot Council School at 5 to join Mrs Robinson's reception class. Early memory of the class being given a food parcel which came from Australia. This was during the war about 1943. The contents of the food parcel were laid out on the classroom floor and we were each given an item to take home. I got a tin of cheese!

I used to like playing on the swings on the rec. I also played a bit of bowls on the rec which was looked after by the green keeper.

When I was 11 I went to Marlcliffe School which meant a tram ride from Neepsend Lane to Middlewood. I lived in the same house until I got married.

Maureen Hunter nee Clixby
Vale Road

Mr & Mrs. Clixby lived on Vale Road with Two Sons Bill & Derek, and three daughters Maureen & Twins Margaret & Eileen.
Mr Clixby & the two sons all worked at the Hallamshire Steel & File Co.

Above Left Bill Clixby senior at work in the Billet yard on Wallace Rd and right his Pigeon cote.

Below George Hunter Maureen's Husband in National Service uniform and right 2015 sisters at reunion Eileen and Maureen with Barbara Warsop.

Terry Hitchens
Vale Rd

Mr and Mrs George Hitchens lived on vale Rd. They had five children- George, Brian, Terry, Lillian and Allen
Lillian died at birth and Brian was killed very young.

Terry's parents owned the fish and chip shop on Mount Rd at the corner of Vale Rd. The family moved between chip shop and the house on Vale Rd.

They all loved animals especially George junior. He started with guinea pigs and rabbits, racing pigeons, hens and then pigs. Their father had geese and ducks, all in the large back garden on Vale Rd. Later he had Pigsty's further up the hill.

Just after the war while there was still rationing most animals were kept for food but the pigeons were kept for racing. George won many prizes for having the fastest pigeons in the race. Alf Eadon who`s house backed onto Georges used to help George get the pigeons in if George was out, he would take the ring from the pigeons leg and put it in the time box. He did this because he knew when George had a pig slaughtered he would get a nice piece of Pork.

Later George moved to a farm near Holmfirth.

Terry and Wife Annett

above Terry

Below left George Hitchens with David right Mr and Mrs Hitchens and Family.

Hillfoot School Football Team
with Terry centre front.

Below: left Terry with his brother Allan

My Life on Parkwood Springs
By Barbara Lee (nee Pierce) 2014

I was born at the City General Hospital, Sheffield (now Northern General) in December 1946. My mum and dad were Fred and Beattie Pierce who lived at 1/4 Wallace Road.

Our house was back-to-back with a shared toilet with the family who lived on the street side. It was 3-storeys high with a living/kitchen area, one bedroom and an attic. There was a sink with a cold water tap in the corner by the window and an oven/fireplace. One internal door led down to the coal cellar and another up to the bedroom and attic. It was always cold upstairs so you didn't linger very long over getting dressed and off to school.

There were 16 other families in the yard and so numerous children of my age and older. We had some great times and were never bored as there was always someone playing out and lots going on.
We used to annoy the neighbours when we put on our metal-wheeled roller skates and clattered up and down the entry.

St Michael's Vicarage would host a weekly film show; the cost was, I think, 2d which included a cup of tea and a biscuit and if finances allowed this is where lots of us used to meet up.

Those kids lucky enough to own a scooter would walk up to the top of Vale Road – which was quite a climb – and then whiz down into Douglas Road. Sometimes they would have a passenger – either standing or sitting!!
My mum used to have a fit at me when I would come home filthy dirty having spent all day sliding up and down the shale stacks left from the quarry working.
Sunday night at our house was bath night – when the small zinc bath would be set in front of the fire and filled with kettle upon kettle of hot water. It took ages to get enough water and then of course it had to be dragged outside to be emptied!!
Joy of joys – the first family to get a television were the Willis's and all us kids used to cram in their one small living room to watch. Sometimes there were just too many to squeeze in and the disappointed ones would make sure they were first in the queue the next.
We were rehoused up to Sheffield Lane Top in about 1967 and though the new property was much larger and modern with a separate kitchen, a bathroom, an indoor loo and a large garden it never quite matched up to the old back-to-back on 'the Springs'.

Below Right, Barbara Lee, Beryl Shaw, Glynis Bird.

Front L to R George lamb, seated Ivy Lamb, Tessie "Landlady" Tom Rooker, behind
George Lamb, Sam the landlord, Right hand side Ernest "Jumbo" Anderson, behind Tom
Rooker, Billy Green, Behind him Bill Hewitt   and "Randy" the dog in front.

Tony Lamb
Wallace Road

Tony lived with his Mum and Dad and sister Margaret.
His sister Margaret died very young at 29 years of age.

Tony has just a few lines to say about his Uncle Stanley who left Parkwood Springs for
WW2 and didn`t come home.

Stanley Rooker born 4-6-1923 and lived at 22, Wallace Rd with his Parents (Tom and
Mary Rooker), 4 brothers and a sister (my Mother - Ivy Rooker) .
Stan was the youngest of 6 children.

He attended Neepsend School and worked at Darwins before joining the Royal Navy.

Stanley was Killed on 20-3-1945 on the Arctic convoys to Russia when his Ship (HMS
Lapwing), a destroyer was torpedoed.
"Anyone going into the sea in them icy waters stood no chance of survival".

It was on the 10th March 1945, just before the end of the war in Europe aged just 21
years, when he wrote his final letter to his Parents.

The last part of his letter read:-
This letter will very probably be the last for a while, but don`t worry Ma, I shall be seeing
you soon
And having the odd drink in the "Parkwood. I must close now. Keep smiling. Cheerio
Ma,

Cheerio Dad, Cheerio all.
Your loving Son.
Stan.

His Girlfriend wrote in the Sheffield Telegraph and Star Newspapers.
He had no enemy,
He feared no Man,
He died for his Country,
As only a hero can.

HMS LAPWING

Stan Rooker 4th from left second row from bottom
Kitty Molloy 3rd from right second row from top

Left below, Stan playing the accordion and right Stan with his Granddad Tom Rooker.

Left to right Tony Lamb in Blackpool, Margaret Lamb on Wallace Rd with Brick works in back ground, Margaret & Tony Lamb with Granddad Tom Rooker in yard on Wallace Road.

Margaret Lamb at Neepsend Lane Tram Stop with shops in the background on
Boyland Street, Neepsend School is on the right.
(Neepsend Church of England School)
Not to be confused with Neepsend School which became Hillfoot County School?

Iris Middleton
Canada
Via face book friends 2015

Iris is 92 years young and used to live on Wallace Road from 1930 to 1946.
She was 5years old when her parents move there and remembers the Bentleys,
Cartwright's and a few more people. She also remembers Danks chip shop just above
the railway arch on Douglas Road.

Iris went to Neepsend School Boyland Street and her Brothers went to Hillfoot School.
Her Father worked on the railway.

Iris lost track of the neighbourhood of Parkwood Springs once she left to join her
Canadian husband in Canada.

Iris returned with her Son, Brian for a visit in the 1956.
Brian remembers going to Hillfoot School while they were visiting and was in Miss
Buxtons class.

I found Iris by chance on the social network of Face Book.
Her Son is very proud of Iris mastering the internet at 92 years of age.
What an achievement.

Robert Page
Wallace Rd

Above Lewis Page my dad in training School Uniform

I lived with my Mum and Dad, Lewis and Nancy Page on Wallace Road

My Father Lewis Page was a sailor in the Second World War.
He trained on HMS Collingwood a land based training school prior to joining his ship,
He sailed on HMS Viceroy. A destroyer on the North Atlantic runs, a company supply ship.

The Captain was Lord David Trentham
My dad was a leading seaman steward to Lord Trentham.
The Viceroy Sank a U boat and recovered a case of brandy which was sent to Winston Churchill.
Churchill sent all the sailors aboard the Viceroy a thank you letter.

Robert remembers his father telling him of the mischief they got up to as children. All the houses on Wallace Road had cellar grates on the pavement to allow the coal delivery Lorries to drop the coal straight into the cellars.
The children went around collecting people's cats and dropping them in Mrs Rooker's cellar; so that when she opened the cellar door all the sooty cats would run out.

David Peacock
3 Douglas Rd

Coincidences:
Danks fish and chip shop was the first place under the railway arch.
I moved into 3, Douglas Rd with my parents in 1944, next door to the chip shop so I think its fare to say we lived at the first house on Parkwood Springs.
In 1957 we moved again to the beer off at the corner of Wallace Rd and Douglas Rd.
The retiring shopkeeper Charlie Watson was a bit of a John Bull not best known for his

customer care.

We left the shop about 1959 and moved to the Manor estate where I eventually got married.

In 1982 I moved to Handsworth. After about two years I got talking to my new neighbours Connie and Douglas. It came to light that in 1944 Connie had lived at no3 Douglas Rd with her granddad and as they moved out we moved in. What a small world. I had many a happy hours playing on Parkwood Springs and made some very good friends who are still friends to this day.

Audrey Proctor nee Pollard
Australia.

Our family name is Pollard, and I was born in Vale Road on the 14th November 1923. I was 15 months old when my mother died, after giving birth to my brother Billy.

My father remarried 3 years later.

We moved to Pickering Road, and lived in the same yard as my grandparents, (Walter and Harriet Pollard). They lived most of their lives at Parkwood Springs. They lived at the very last house on Pickering Road

In 1945 I married Harry Proctor the coal merchant's son and Left Parkwood Springs. We lived at Intake for a while until we immigrated to Australia in 1952, with our four small children. We have all had a wonderful life in Australia.

Bill Ronksley

I worked at the Neepsend Locomotive Depot at the bottom of Douglas Rd, Parkwood Springs, from 1939 where my Trade Union branch of ASLEF, was founded in April 1880. Workers employed in many different industries also resided in Parkwood Springs and many of them were active Trade Union Members.

The Railway was an extremely important centre in Sheffield and the local Parkwood Springs depot was a colony and all their workers were solid labour supporters. Some of them became Labour councillors.

Herbert Bates a railway man held Communist party meetings in his house on Wallace Road.

Parkwood Springs became a conditional residential area for rail workers because of employer insistence. In other words, to always be "on call" they had to live within what was known as a "calling up area".

At the top of Wallace Road there was a lodging house for their workers. The railway had to deliver all the goods needed for it, bedding, furniture, cutlery and food.

Smith's strikers at Parkwood Engine shed 1920s.
Courtesy Sheffield Library and archives.

The Wonderful thing about the people of Parkwood Springs was that there was a tie between them all. I was very impressed with Community Spirit.
Many of the local residents were very active in the Rutland Hall Settlement, and were educated in Local politics, local choirs, and Esperanto group plus local sport.
During the Blitz lots of shops in the city burnt down due to lack of observation. So it became compulsory for the railway workers on Parkwood to do fire watch duty after working a 12 hour shift.
They found out that the shop managers living outside the area were not included so all the drivers went on strike about it and they were taken to court for ignoring the fire rota and were charged a penny a piece but crowds of supporters outside the court house threw in there pennies in support of the rail workers.

Also during the blitz as soon as the gas pressure went down from the gas lamps all the pipes underground blow up all along the pavement to the wicker.

There were so many trains during the war that they would be queuing in the sidings and Trains were held up hours to allow trains with troops to get through. I was 17 at the time and had been on one of these trains held up and my Mother wondered what had happened to me.

Engines were repaired in the sheds and on Monday mornings in the sidings at Parkwood locomotive depot 20 trains were all fired simultaneously and clouds of black smoke poured out over the land and spread according to the wind direction.

A lot of railways employees came over the Penines from Manchester and settled here, quit a few of them were Irish.
An Irish train driver built a fairy Castle behind the platform of Neepsend Station and all the staff cared for it even though it had nothing to do with the railway.

During the war the homeless down and out people were allowed to sleep on the barrows in the brickyard. The Bricks were of a very high quality. Some bricks were supplied to local builders in Stannington.
The local gamekeeper used to mash his tea in the Engine sheds.

During the war one of the Railway drivers who had been off work with heart failure, was at the top of Douglas Road when they set off the Rocket Guns simultaneously with no air raid warning, he thought he was going to die.
At the top of Parkwood Springs there were anti aircraft guns; later on during the war they changed from Ack- Ack guns to Rocket guns which would shoot simultaneously in all directions to detract the Germans. These Rockets were lighter and could be fired by Women.

My granddad had the pork shop (W H Swannack) and abattoir on Langsett Road at the top of Wood Street very popular with Parkwood Springer's and mother new all the Parkwood Springs customers very well.

William Herbert Swannack, Pork Butcher,
and
Doris Swannack, Daughter.
10th October, 1916.

Russell Self
51 Douglas Road.

Russell was born on Parkwood Springs in 1948. He left the area in 1969 to start a job in another town. Russell went to Hillfoot county school, and then to Chaucer school until he left in 1963.

The family moved to Parkwood Springs after 1908, and lived at the top Wallace Road. Russell grandfather Charles took a job as a labourer at the gas works, and later became a shop steward, and a father of 12 children.
The house was so small that they had to have two sittings for Sunday lunch. (There is a family story of forming a chain to get the dishes from the table to the sink and back into the cupboard.

Roy Smith.
Wallace Road

Left Roy right Mr. & Mrs Smith with Roy & wife Pat.

Roy Smith was born on Wallace Rd 1936 and lived there until the slum clearance.

His dad worked at Hallamshire Steel and File Co.   Roy worked at Slack and Sellers. Owned by Stewart Goodwin, on Mowbray St Neepsend
He was a smither.

During the really bad winter of 1947 our School stayed open, all the Children never had a day off.
He remembers climbing over the wall at the back of his house as a short cut to get to the shop on Pickering Rd and as he was climbing he fell off and broke both his wrists. He never told his mother how he fell and she never found out.

Roy kept and raced pigeons when he was about 14 years old and had them until he was called up for National Service.

His brother Trevor Smith was landlord of Parkwood Pub at the bottom of Douglas Rd for a while.

The Local Midwife lived opposite them.
A Woman called Lizzie always stood outside her front door to nosy at everyone who passed.

Sandra Smyth nee Moody
Douglas Rd.

We lived with my grandparents Mr and Mrs J Shaw on Douglas Rd where I was born; I have a brother and Sister Molly and John. We had a very loving upbringing. I liked living Parkwood Springs.
We did tap dancing in an attic at the top of Vale Rd next to the chip shop I think.
There were quite a lot of lads and lasses that met on the swings or to play rounder's. A few of us walked to Shireclife or Shiregreen. There was a right gang of us who played on the wood where we found an old air raid shelter from the war time inside it was all smelly and horrible.
I loved playing the piano. My Granddad Shaw taught me how to play the organ with the bellows; I had to feet them.
I remember seeing and listening to a chap playing the bagpipes opposite the Douglas Inn I wondered if anyone else remembers this.

My father wrote a diary about his time working on the railway.

Excerpts from
Bradford to Sheffield
Diary of a Railwayman
By Driver Len Moody

Len was born in Bradford 5th January 1920
On leaving school he got a job on the railway. Notes went up in his depot asking for volunteers to go to Sheffield so Len volunteered and was transferred to Neepsend loco sheds, Sheffield in June 1941.
The foreman had an address of someone who was willing to take in lodgers and sent for a driver to show him where it was. When they got there the house was in ruins only the outside toilets were left standing.
They wondered around and eventually found someone prepared to take them in. It was a large terraced house and there were fourteen lodgers. In the bedroom were four beds with just enough room to pass between our belongings were kept in our cases under the bed. All the houses had black out blinds over the windows because of the heavy bombings. The landlady would leave them bread and butter and bacon to fry for themselves. One morning when they got up there was nothing to eat and no tea to mash. One of the lodgers a scruffy chap had been with a woman all night and given her their breakfast. At Sunday lunch they all had to sit on a plank.

He was describing the situation to the timekeeper at the loco sheds and he suggested that he go to a drivers widow who lived just outside the engine sheds on Parkwood

Springs. I thought what a nice sounding area, but in fact it was the dirtiest place I had ever seen. It was like a small village the only entrance being the small railway arch. Below the arch was the rolling mill. On top of the furnaces there were large boxes to prevent the German pilots from seeing the flames. There was always dense black smoke coming out of these boxes and it used to roll up the hill like a fog covering the windows with grime. The area had been heavily bombed. The first time I saw it I thought that I could never live there but as it turned out I was wrong. Anyhow it was the better of the two evils and Mrs Dowse agreed to take two of us in. My railway work carried on and the shifts were very varied.

Mrs Dowse being an old lady with bad eyesight looked after us as best she could, but because of rationing didn't do too well at the shops. We were hungry and didn't get enough to eat; unlike the steel workers we had no canteen to provide food.

One day when working on a train to Annsley my co driver turned up with a box that they had broke open, it was full of prunes: His mate took some home with him stuffing his haversack, I did not take any for Mrs Dowse as she might not approve but I ate a lot and soon regretted it as they gave me terrible stomach ache. I suppose you could say I got my just desserts.
When I lodged with Mrs Dowse I met a girl who lived in the next yard. I used to admire her long dark hair. She was to become my wife.
Mrs Dowse was not quite capable of looking after us so I found lodgings at Wisewood with a chap who was a butcher at the co-op so I was well looked after there.

By 1943 the whole of the outdated locomotive depot at Neepsend was transferred to a brand new depot at Darnell.
That same year I married Madge who had lived in the next yard on Parkwood Springs. Because of rationing I had to borrow a suit from a relative to get married in. With not much money we had to live with her parents so I ended up back on Parkwood Springs. My father in law was a very generous man; he also worked on the railway.

My wife's mother was one on her own, very old fashioned and afraid of electricity. She used to wash clothes in the old copper boiler and cook on an old black lead range fireplace. She would not have an electric washer or iron but instead had the old flat iron that had to be heated on the fire or gas ring. She spent every Friday morning polishing the black lead fireplace until it shone.

On the 16th February 1944 our very first Daughter Sandra was born. We were passing through a rough period as income tax had to be paid on the previous six months pay so I was taxed as a single man and money was very tight. When Sandra was born there was no National Health Service. We thought it best to have a doctor to attend the birth. When she was born the doctor could not be contacted so we had to send for the welfare for assistance and two very young nurses came out in an emergency to deliver our baby. I had a beautiful light haired daughter. The doctor still sent his bill. As soon as she was born we were entitled to orange juice and cod liver oil from the welfare.

Roger Simcox
Parkwood Rd

Roger remembers helping to dig and build up a well on Mount Rd near the Douglas Inn

Below Roger left with Roy Smith showing us the winter warmers made for his son in the 1960`s at one of our reunions. All the men wanted to light them there and then and went outside to have a go causing much laughter 2016.

Pat Rowbotham (nee Spencer)
Pickering Rd

Three generations of the Spencer family lived on Parkwood Springs, mostly on Pickering Rd.
Pats parents were Mr Joe Spencer and Janet Sherwood Spencer nee Johnson.
They had 3 children, Victor, Pat and Janet.
Joe worked for Sheffield City Council he collected Firms waste for Destruction.
Mrs Spencer worked for G W Waugh's on Douglas Rd.
She drove a lorry delivering mineral water to customers.

One relative of the family moved to Langsett Rd area because their house was bombed at the bottom of Pickering Rd.

Pat was born in 1933 and remembers the war very well. She was terrified when in the middle of the night the sirens went off. Her Mum used to say to her after trying to wake Pat to go to the shelter. "You go to sleep to die" because Pat couldn't wake up easily. It was terrible to be woken out of your sleep to go in a very cold and wet shelter.
Because of the hill we all lived on, our gardens were all terraced. Their shelter was down the lower part of the garden and full of water around their feet. So her Mum arranged for them to go in a friend's shelter but that did not work out because of the cramped space. So they moved to a shelter on the recreation ground which lots of families used.
This was much better and Pat felt safe there. It became a nice experience as they sang songs or told stories. The parents made the best of that terrible situation.

As a child she remembers being bathed in the sink.

The children went to older neighbours to ask if they could do them any shopping, not always getting a good response.

Pat loved living on Parkwood Springs as everyone new one another and the community was a very friendly one.
Her best friend was Joan Winks who used to live on Vale Rd and who she still keeps in touch with.

Blanchard's was her first place of work in the hat dept. she loved that job.
Then moved to Millhouses where they made ladies underwear.
And later still to Neepsend works where they made springs.
She was quite feisty and always stood up for herself even at a very young age.

Pat met her husband at Hillfoot County School youth club in the 1950s
After marrying they lived with her Mum and Dad for a while on Pickering Rd. They had two Children David and Judith. They then moved to a large house at the top of Pickering Road and had their youngest son Anthony. They then moved to Burn Cross where Pat lives now.

While Pat was pregnant with Judith she had a craving for Hulleys Ice Cream Who delivered ices up Parkwood Springs.
Judith ended up marrying the eldest son of the Hulleys Family.
Was her craving Clairvoyant?

Raymond Swift
Mount Road

Lived with his parents and Sister Pauline at 22 Mount Rd from 1938 until 1963 when he moved with his wife Jean to Shireclife. Ray`s parents remained on there until the very end of housing on Parkwood Springs. This was very distressing for them surrounded by derelict properties. His father held onto his house until the later 1970`s because he wanted to choose where he was being moved to and stuck to his principles until he got the house he wanted.

As a boy Ray remembers boy's feuds between boys from Wallace Rd and where he lived on Mount Rd
He must have said something about the boys on Wallace Rd that they did not like so when they got him alone they ganged up on him and set about him beating him, so he went home in a mess with his clothes all dirty. His Father asked him what had happened and he made up some excuse about the state of his clothes.
But his Father made him tell the truth.
Then his Father marched him down to Wallace Rd to show him how to stick up for himself.
And said who are these boys show me. Well Raymond did not like to say who it was as he didn't want any more repercussions from those bully's, so he looked for a very small boy and said it was him. His Father said to him now go and hit him, very embarrassing for Ray.

Ray and Sister Pauline

Ray 2014

Terry Turner
Vale Road

Originally Terry lived with his family on Mount Road and after the blitz they moved to Vale Road.

He had two older Sisters an older Brother and a younger Brother Tony.

In the 1930s Terry remembers Shrove Tuesday being "Scramble Day" on Parkwood Springs.

At the beginning of the religious festival of Lent the congregation had to give up "fats and sugar" for the month.

The shop keepers Bownes, Tingles, Woodalls, Watsons, and Nixon's paper shop decided to carry on with the tradition to give the children a treat.

On Scramble Day they would throw out the door wrapped sweats and a few coins, ½ and 1 pennies and the children had to scramble for them on the pavement all very good fun. This tradition ended when WW11 started

Above reunion 2015.
Terry standing with Roger Simcox sat left and Barry Robinson sat right

Connie Walters (nee Bentley)
120 Pickering Road

She was born at Lime St in 1922.
Her Family moved to Parkwood Springs in 1929.their house was across the road from the shop at the top of the genel.
The shopkeeper at the time was Mr Torry. Later the shop belonged to Mrs Bownes.

Connie`s Mother worked at Moore and Wright and her father worked on Mowbray St.
At 92 Years old she has a very good memory of living up Parkwood Springs.
Connie attended The Church School, Neepsend.

She remembers being in Service at 16 year of age, and travelled to Ecclesall to work for a family there. Her uniform was a Green Dress and a White Apron, a White Cap and cuffs for every day and for later in the evening A Black Dress with the White accessories. Her salary was 12/6 per week plus good food.

Connie walked to school in the morning and came home lunch time so that she could deliver a basket of Stew or Meat and Potato pie made by Mrs Knowles for her Sons, two brothers who lived near to her who worked in Sheffield and had to be careful not to spill any on the way. She walked down the hill with the basket to catch the Tram to Fitzalan Square for ½ pence and onto a little Mesters on Sycamore St. Left the basket in the time office came home for lunch walked back to School for the Afternoon and then home for tea.

Another thing she remembered was Bowne's Shop at the top of Pickering Rd getting Outspan Oranges delivered in large wooden Boxes 3 foot long and 20ins wide that were tied up with string made of Raffia and which the children begged, and tied together to make a skipping rope that reached across the road.
They also used this string to swing from the gas lamps. The lamplighter Mr Pollard lived near her. He carried his ladder over his shoulder around Parkwood Springs in order for him to light the gas.

There was a chip shop on Pickering Rd Opposite Mount Rd. William Moor's locally known as Piggy Moors because he also kept pigs, he had an Alsatian guard dog that everyone was scared of. Another family Falcon`s also kept Pigs.

Bin Men came to empty bins of Ashes from the fire; this was most of the waste at that time as people burnt most of their rubbish.

The night of the Blitz she was in the Empire Cinema and remembers it well.
They went into the cellar and was stuck there until the all clear siren went off.

During the time she spent on Parkwood Springs she used to have Piano lessons at the chapel on Douglas Rd, The Piano Teachers name was Vera Quibble.
Connie`s friends were Joyce Fisher, Vale Rd, Irene Knowles, Wallace Rd,
Another friend of hers lived next door to Jack Addison. And across the Rd was Jessie Pashley.
Her Mother bought her a "Sit up and Beg Bike" She remembered buying a pair of stockings from a shop on Harvest lane that cost 6d. (Old money)

There were three very large houses at the top of Pickering Rd. The gas manager's house was the first above the genel where in the 1920s Mr and Mrs Wild lived, with their daughter Mona.

The Blackwell's lived in the next house. At one time the owners of that house must have had horses as there were stables in the yard but no horses.

George Torry, joiner and family lived in the very last house on Pickering Rd. Son George managed the beer off on Mount Rd for a while.

Dora Woodhead their daughter opened their front room as hairdressers.

Hairdresser's 1940-50s

I remember Dora Woodhead doing the very first Kalinin perm. (See Kalinin perm web site)

I decided to have one of these perms.

It was a heated permanent wave using permanent wave solution and a machine that was similar to an electric hair drier but at the top were circular electrical heated bars that could hold Bakelite hair grips to be heated. When having a perm with this method the hair was wound around the curlers and then gripped with the heated grips making your head top heavy. The perm was wonderful and lasted for ages. This kind of perm did not last for long; I think it must have been because of the weight of the curlers on your head.

Mrs Muriel Parkin also did hairdressing in her front room on Vale Rd.

Dave White
Mount Road

Left Dave with Roy Smith

Dave has a very good memory of living at Parkwood and has lots of stories.

At the oral history day we spent with the Archaeology Students from Sheffield University. He said you had to be careful what you said about people on Parkwood because we were all related one way or another.

He remembers the journey to school down the station steps which were all made from railway sleepers and on to Hoyland Road Neepsend.

Passing the many coal drops along Hoyland Road power station, one day they all dropped and tons of coal fell across the road and a path had to be cleared for the school children to pass to get to school.

On the hillside behind the old railway station of around 1910 someone in the past had Built a fairy castle with glass windows and everything and lots of children crossed the line to see it and spent ages looking at it. It would be still there today but for the clay falling in front of it.

Dave's Grandparents told him about the gamekeeper of Parkwood Springs called George Broom who walked to Herries Road to the cinema over the path called brooms path later called the cinder track. George Broom also left his gun propped up outside the Douglas Inn to go and play dominoes.
The Gamekeeper also mashed his Tea in the Engine sheds which at that time were still surrounded with trees.

During the time he lived there he saw a London trolley bus on Mount Road and was mystified as to how it got there, it must have come over Brooms path as no way would it could have got under the bridge on Bardwell Road.
(Dave's quote get that darn brooms path nobdy knows abaat that naa)

He told us that when the Hallamshire retired their Shire Horses he saw a long line of them all tethered together walking up Douglas Road.
Dave himself kept some horses.
During the war there were 3 water tanks on Parkwood Springs, one on the recreation ground, one on Douglas Terrace and one on Wallace Road because if Bardwell Road bridge got bombed the emergency services would have been cut off.

It was a fun place to live with lots going on.
Some rogues lived there also.
A long time ago a rogue hid away from police on Parkwood Springs for a while, because this criminal had shot a police Man somewhere down south.

Above top left coal drops 1940s and right the remains 2016.

Left Neepsend station footbridge and right station steps from Parkwood Springs

Patricia Woodhouse (nee Higgins)
Wallace Road

My story starts when Alice and Frederick Higgins went to live at Parkwood Springs. They lived on Wallace Road across from Pickering Road until their house was destroyed by a bomb. Due to this they were rehoused to Wallace Road next to the corner shop owned by the "Watsons".

I was born in 1943 and lived there until I married in 1962. I had one younger sister Christine.

The yard had 16 houses in it. It started under the arch in Douglas Road next to the Chip Shop and went around the corner on to Wallace Road. Three of the houses had hen huts.

The other families living in the Yard were: Peacocks, Fosters, Rookes, Bebingtons, Lindleys, Watsons, Stances, Higgins, Phoenix, Kelly Cowens, Barrats, Pearce, Russell, Woodhouse and Birds. I married Alan Woodhouse who lived at number 9 Wallace Road. Joe and Doris Woodhouse, my in-laws, were well known as Joe had lived in number 7 Wallace Road as a child.

As you can imagine there was plenty of children to play with. In the summer Mr Peacock would put a hosepipe to his cold water tap an all the children ran for their costumes. We ran in and out of the water and thought it was magic! In November all of the residents would bring fireworks and food. Stools and chairs were placed in a circle around a large bonfire which seemed to stay alight all night.

I went to Sunday school on Douglas Road. Miss Fretwell was our teacher and Mr Bailey played the piano. I had a card which was stamped with a star. At the end of term you would be given a book for good attendance. I always remember one book "Ching the doll nobody loved". I loved it.

We would play in the wood taking with us a bottle of water and some bread and jam for a picnic. Everyone drank from the glass pop bottle and the last person got all of the crumbs in the bottom. When the bottle was empty we would go to the nearest house on Douglas Road to get it filled again. We would spend most of the mornings in the wood or the rec. We had an allotment next to the bowling green. Mam and dad would work on it whilst my sister and I played on the swings – no thought was ever given to us straying and we never did.

My father and father-in-law both worked on the railway. The trains ran along the bottom of our yard and as they passed the windows would rattle. Once a goods wagon came off the rails and rolled down the embankment. If we went away the neighbours all knew and would wave to us on the train and again when we came back. In the war years the railway men would throw lumps of coal off the wagon and the neighbours would go and get them from the embankment.

After I married Alan Woodhouse in 1962 we moved to Crookes. We returned to Parkwood Springs to visit our parents but most of the children had moved on and contact was lost.
Then 37 years later I met Tony Lamb. We decided to try and contact our old friends. Obviously this time the ski village had been built on the site where we used to live therefore we enquired if we could hire a room for 20 people for a reunion.
We advertised on Radio Sheffield and in the Sheffield Star. Not only did we find our old friends but also 550 others – we ended up hiring the whole of the ski village for the reunion.
The night was magical as the response was fantastic – much better than we could ever have imagined.
It just goes to prove how great Parkwood Springs was to live in. Everyone who attended said the same thing.
Just close your eyes and you are back again in your childhood roaming the hills. I loved it.

Back row Tony Lamb 2nd from left Pat 3rd David 4th Below Pats sister Christine centre.

Below 1999 excerpt from Sheffield Newspapers.

The road back: Pat Woodhouse, who organised a reunion of ex-residents of Parkwood Springs, and, inset, a map of the area.

A lift in store as lost villagers meet on ski slope and slip into the past

Jillian Ward

MEMORIES of a lost village on the edge of Sheffield city centre will come flooding back when former residents hold the first reunion since the houses were demolished 25 years ago.

Pat Woodhouse, who was born in Parkwood Springs, says she has been surprised by the response to her call for a reunion of ex-villagers.

"Within a day of going on local radio about the reunion I'd received 60

calls from former residents who were delighted at the idea of reliving old times," she said.

"Parkwood was a village in its own right and was a very tight-knit community. The residents were scattered all over Sheffield when the houses were demolished and I felt it was time we all met up again."

The reunion will be held on November 6 at the club house of Sheffield's Ski Village, which was built on the site of Parkwood Springs.

New attraction: Sheffield's Ski Village, built on the site of Parkwood Springs.

Pat was also a friend of Mavis Mitchell who lived in a very large house on Vale Road just below the vicarage.
Pat has kept in touch with Mavis for all these years, and is still in touch with today.

Mr and Mrs Mitchell had a family of ten children five boys and five girls.
The girls moved to places far apart when they married.
In fact all the family have moved far apart.

Mavis was one of the babes in the Panto" Babes in the Wood".
Ralph and Terry Mitchell belonged to St Michaels youth club.

L to R is the Mitchell girls, Doreen, Mavis, Rose, Olive and Annie.
Excerpt from Sheffield News papers.

Friends of Parkwood Springs

1965. Ray Swift was now living on Shireclife. Building was going on all around them and he became involved along with neighbours there because of unsuitable high rise buildings that were going to take place by "Sheffield City Council" very near to him which would have shut out all his light. He set up a meeting with the Town Hall, City Councillors to object to this. The tenants had been informed that the buildings were going to be Garages. High Rise flats were not on the plans. So they fought this, meeting up with the Councillors and the Ombudsman to stop the high rise building, they won and houses were built instead.

Jean Armstrong a neighbour of Rays organised a group of people to meet at her house, because also there was a terrible smell coming off Parkwood Springs Land fill site that had to be dealt with because of health reasons. They set up meetings with the Council and residents of Shireclife to do something about the landfill site and from that they got a liaison set up with Sheffield City Councillors which remains today to sort out problems with the tip. Which now belongs to Viridor?

Between the years of moving from Parkwood to Shireclife many buildings had taken place.
Parkwood Collage had been built on Shireclife, and Later in the 1980`s the Ski Slope was built and an adventure Playground.

By 2000 plus all these buildings were being demolished yet again.
The Residents Group began to change and evolved.
The Group became Parkwood Springs Steering Group.
Who were local residents, members of Parkwood landfill action group and the Ramblers Association, officers from Sheffield City Council`s Parks and Countryside Service and the Wildlife Trust.
Because the Parkwood Springs Steering Group wasn`t a membership group.

In 2010 The Group was formally set up to become
Friends of Parkwood Springs
2016 Aims
1: Are to protect and conserve the wildlife and the Environment of the green space of
Parkwood Springs
2: To work towards improving the green space as a resource for local residents and the
Sheffield City Council.
3: To encourage responsible use of the Natural Environment that Parkwood Springs
Offers.
 To promoting conservation of the area`s wildlife, geological and historical heritage,
organising improvements to paths and access areas.
Two full size football pitches were left from the days of the Collage, and now used well
Sporting Event, Schools Activities, family and cultural events, are all taking place now.
There is now a mountain Bike Trail and a spectacular Autumn Beacons project.
Wild life and Bat watch, Dawn chorus have been organised.
We need Parkwood to go back to the original Parkwood it started as and make it into a
Park to be enjoyed by all in the centre of Sheffield.

My Epitaph to Parkwood Springs 2016

I think that what has become clear about the time we lived on Parkwood Springs
i.e.; After the war, late 1940`s to 1960`s
Is that we are all of the opinion that it was the best time to be a child, being free from the
pressures of today.
We did not have the possessions of today. We learned how to share.
With the worry of the war behind us we were free.
We had to make our own fun and play together outside.
We got very dirty and learned how to mix with one another, learning vital skills of life and
how to communicate with one another.
The Community Spirit was wonderful, because of the closed position of Parkwood Springs
we were one big Happy Family.   Even after 50 years we still have that Community Spirit.
In our minds eye, our home is still on Parkwood Springs, which is why we still love our
reunions.
As soon as we are together again, there is nonstop chatter and laughter about the
wonderful times we had together.

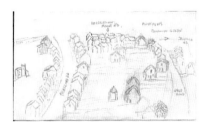 

See far left Castle House.   My house in the centre.
Pickering Road left and on the right Vale Road.

By Barbara Warsop (Drawn from website "Britain from Above")

The next items are photocopies of the Parkwood Echo of 1971
This records the trauma and disruptions to lives during the
slum clearances.

PARKWOOD ECHO

1906
Old Park Wood

1971
Slum

WHAT'S NEXT ?
Redevelopment ? as light-industry, housing,
. . . . . or as a tip?

The "Parkwood Echo" "courtesy of Pete Addison" shows the turmoil of what happens
when a Community of People is being destroyed.

Dominoes ..... that could kill

The Vicarage in Vale Road stood empty and abandoned for years before it was broken into and the contents ripped out. As a result of angry protests from mothers, concerned about their childrens' safety should they play near, or in the Vicarage, the Corporation has pulled down the top floor, making it more dangerous than before.

Meanwhile, next door, people move out and the process of decay begins again, creating another death trap.

Top picture; the Vicarage was a beautiful big house on Vale Rd.

74

FOCUS ON

PARKWOOD SPRINGS - 'The Forgotten Village'

Our Contact reporter interviews Mr. George Ellis, the Secretary of the Parkwood Springs Community House. He has lived in the village—now a part of the Pitsmoor Parish—for the past 38 years. He is married with a young family.

What was Parkwood Springs like in the past?

A thriving little community of no more than 3,000 souls. The Church then played a prominent part in the social life of the district with the local chapel. In those days we had a full time parson living in the community in the St. Michael's Vicarage in Vale Road.

The Recreation ground was a good sports attraction and all the allotments were taken and carefully tended.

I can remember the time when one could walk from the Springs to Ecclesfield without passing through a built up area—that was by going over the hills. Somehow the area never seemed finished. The roads never got anywhere!

What caused the area to become so run down?

It began in the war when something like a quarter of the housing went through the bombing. After the war the houses were not rebuilt, instead the empty spaces were used by industry or just left derelict.

In 1957 we were earmarked by the Corporation for Redevelopment which meant that people lost pride in their houses—as they could be moved at any time. As time went by folk just lost heart.

On top of this problem families were dumped upon the community, or they just moved in as the housing was so cheap. The natives of the area did not know how to cope with this inflow.

No decent people would now think of moving in among us.

How do people feel about the present situation?

A number of us are resentful because we feel the Council have let us down. There has been untold delay in producing any plan for the area. It is amazing that the City ignores such a good site for redevelopment so near to the City Centre. Instead we are left to rot.

Is there still a strong Community life?

Certainly many who move away from the Springs tell us how much they miss the community life. Often the new estate seems cold and unfriendly.

We try and keep the community spirit alive, even against so many odds. There are three places that life still revolves around—besides the local pubs. That is Hillfoot school—that has been promised to be left for us as long as it is needed. The Methodist Chapel and our Community house in Mount Road.

How soon will depopulation take place?

Already folk are moving out. The Community is now only about 1,000. The Housing Department are offering some folk keys but cannot promise to clear the area until the end of 1975. Then only five houses will be left, according to the Ministry of the Environment.

Anything you feel strongly about?

Yes. I am sure the rebuilding of houses with the industry is within the realms of possibility still. The argument that there is no second access road is very weak. Either a road could be cut from Cookswood across the hill or the road over the railway could be strengthened. Once the vision is caught of what our Parkwood village could become, all the so called problems would be dealt with.

Why should people be made to move out to Mosborough when we could live right close to the City Centre and to our work. We want some planner or Councillor to catch a vision of what could be, and then have the courage to see it through. Many people would back such a man up to the hilt.

PARKWOOD SPRINGS RESIDENTS ACTION ASSOCIATION
GENERAL MEETING WED MAY 12th

A General Meeting has been called, which will be held in the Methodist Chapel, Wallace Road, on Wednesday May 12th, at 7.30p.m. This meeting is essential if the Action Association is to continue. From time to time residents change thier views on various subjects which makes it difficult for the Committee to take the necessary action.

This meeting will give you the opportunity to tell the Committee just what you want and suggest how to go about it.

IS AN ACTION ASSOCIATION NECESSARY IN PARKWOOD SPRINGS?

IS THE COMMITTEE GIVING MUCH ACTION?

HOW CAN YOU THE RESIDENTS HELP!

It is of the utmost importance for you to attend if you consider action is necessary to obtain satisfactory answers from the Corporation, or are you prepared to sit back and wait until they decide.

THE ACTION COMMITTEE

Many people don't know the Action Group Committee, so here is a list of names and addresses. If you have any queries I am sure they will try and help you by bringing it to the attention of the Committee.

Chairman:- Mr. C. Ellis. 113, Pickering Road.
Deputy Chairman:- Mr. H. Carr, 165, Douglas Road.
Treasurer:- Mr. D. Smith, 217, Douglas Road.

Representative for Wallace Road.
    Mr. Williams, 150. Wallace Road.
    Mr. Ward. Wallace Road.
Representative for Vale Road.
    Mrs. Pence, 48, Vale Road.
    Mrs. French, 87, Vale Road.
Representative for Mount Road.
    Mrs. Swift, 22, Mount Road.
    Mr. R. Haywood, 111, Vale Road.
Co-opted Members.

Representative for Pickering Road.
    Mr. A. Eadon, 73, Pickering Road.
    Mr. W. Carrigan, 83, Pickering Road.
Representative for Douglas Road.
    Mrs. W. Ellis, 83, Douglas Road.
    Mr. D. Christain, 50, Douglas Road.

    Mrs. Lovell (Methodist Chapel) Rev. C. Cowper (Christ Church Pitsmoor)
    Mrs. Wass (Social Worker) Mr. Williams (Headmaster Millfoot) Miss. C. Julius
    (Student Representative)

VIEWPOINT

This section is for you to air your views and comments, naturally everything could not be published, so one would have to be discreet.

OTHER ITEMS of topical interest and news of Births, Deaths etc., are welcome along with recipes and For Sale ads.
The above items must be recieved at Community House, before the 3rd Wednesday in the month.

OBITUARY
It is with regret that we hear of the deaths of Mrs. Chamberlain, late of Parkwood Springs who died on a visit to the district, also Mr. W. Brooks of Wallace Road. To their families we extend our sincere condolences.

PARKWOOD ECHO
THE VOICE OF PARKWOOD SPRINGS

No.7.   April, 1971

Dear Friends,

Once more it is Newsletter time and although this months issue does not contain any pictures, I feel sure that you will find it of equal interest as the last issue. Next month the Municipal Elections are held, a time when we elect a representative to serve us on the City Council. Let us hope that the new Council that sits in June will be a little more sympathetic towards us in Parkwood Springs and endevour to try and solve some of our Problems.

G. ELLIS.
Chairman.

PARKWOOD SPRINGS REDEVELOPMENT EXHIBITION

The exhibition which was held in Community House on Thursday 25th March for three days had a reasonable attendance.   About Four hundred people came to see it, with a good number of non-residents from other parts of the City - Gleadless, Firth Park, Millhouses, Pitsmoor to mention only a few.

RESULTS - From comments expressed by residents of the district   over 50% would like to stay if Re-developement was to take place similar to the plans drawn up, some would not commit themselves until further information was at hand.   Ofcourse there was those who definately want to leave the district and here we must stress that most of us want to go if re-developement isn't likely to take place within a reasonable time. Some former residents of the district would like to come back if re-davelopement for housing took place.

We believe that re-developement for housing could commence sometine next year and an early clearance of the area could take place during 1974-75.

REDEVELOPMENT AS A RECREATIONAL AREA

Plans for re-developing PARKWOOD SPRINGS into a Recreational Area including the present residential area right across the allotments and tips to Herries Road, some 270 acres at a nominal sum of £688,000 the plans will be presented to the Council for their official sanction.   The un-official plans (Morning Telegraph) are very vague and it is no doubt at all that by the time they have got round to it, the figure could be almost doubled.

WHERE IS THE MONEY TO COME FROM?   WHOSE GOING TO PAY?

From information at hand the Government will not give a grant for clearing and redeveloping an area unless it is for housing, then 75% grant can to obtained.   The poor old rate payer would once more have to suffer approx. £3 per head of every man, woman and child in the City.   This means additional rates along with other rising costs.   Can we afford it?   Can the City afford it?

May 12th 1971 Extracts from Parkwood Echo.

A report on the general meeting of the Parkwood Springs resident's action association states that it was attended by little over 30 residents.
This was a poor turn out after so much criticism about what the committee was doing. It was intended to get a general view of what the residents thoughts were on what the committee were trying to achieve.
The chairman stated that "it appeared that residents themselves had no interest in moving from the district although they state they do, and it would be this attitude that would hold redevelopment and clearance back and not the committee.
 The committee have been all out to try and get satisfactory answers from the corporation and until such time and clearance did take place they would try and get better conditions for residents e.g. Bus service, a community house and a general clean up of the area.

Community house opened Monday 7th June 1971.

In the survey of February 1970 84% residents would like to leave the Parkwood Springs. Many now have cold feet. Is it fear of higher rents or thoughts of where they might have to go with additional travel expenses?   Sooner or later we will have to face the facts.

A student survey 1971

Volunteers from the student community action contacted and interviewed 260 households, ¾ of the residents of Parkwood Springs.
In its present state 29% of residents would be sorry to leave.
59% would be very pleased to leave.
12% attended a place of worship.
If a doctors surgery was started once or twice a week
48% would transfer to that Doctor 8% were unsure.
Many respondents were interested in what activities would take place in "The Community House". Mount Rd. 58% would support it financially while not attending.
85% Read the Parkwood Echo, 84% read the Sheffield Star.
Only 74% of residents had heard of the residents Action Association.

Only 6% believed that the corporation consulted them enough about their needs or told them enough about what is going to happen. There being a lack of information concerning when and how they are to be rehoused.
If Parkwood springs was redeveloped as housing.
47% would choose to stay 49% would choose to leave, the remainder unsure.

The Reason the council have not informed the residents about what is going to happen to the area, is that they do not know themselves.

WINTER OLYMPICS

All roads lead to Sochi for worldly Woods

Sheffield-born skier going for gold

by Mark Staniforth

FROM Sheffield to Sochi via the southernmost tip of south America, James Woods has traversed the planet in pursuit of his sport and is relishing the prospect of trying to win a Winter Olympic medal.

The 22-year-old Woods has led a nomadic existence since reaching the elite level in ski slopestyle, a freestyle discipline which will be making its debut at the Games in Sochi, Russia, this month with the women's event on February 11 and the men two days later.

Woods has slept at home just five nights in the past year and since winning his first World Cup in Ushuaia on the tip of Tierra del Fuego, has found himself thrust into the spotlight as one of Great Britain's best prospects for Olympic gold.

But at the root of his success is not some distant glacial paradise but the old toothbrush-like dry slope at Sheffield Ski Village, which now sulks in his home city as a burned-out and seemingly unretrievable wreck following a fire more than a year ago.

Woods describes the plight of the place where he and Katie Summerhayes, who will also compete in ski slopestyle in Sochi, honed

their skills as "heart-breaking." It is likely to be earmarked for demolition.

Not that it was ever that salubrious: "I was always too cool to ride in anything other than a tee-shirt with no gloves, so it was very sore and your skin could get really cut up if you touched down," Woods said.

The young Woods was quickly the star of the slopes and soon inspired the likes of Summerhayes to share his dream of one day taking part, in those pre-Olympic days, in the prestigious X Games.

"I never even dreamed of going to the Olympics when I was younger and it was all about the X Games," Woods said.

"You couldn't beat it. We were kids messing around outside and having the most fun. It's quite heart-breaking what's happened to the place. It was a good place for kids to go and more than anything it just made me happy."

Woods realised a long-held dream when he won a bronze medal at the Aspen X Games last year and won the overall World Cup title in his discipline as well as a silver medal in the World Championships in Voss.

"The Olympics are a great chance for us to showcase our sport and get more kids involved back home," he said.

A question mark still hangs over the future of the Parkwood Springs area, of Sheffield, residents have been told.

While unfit housing is being cleared, the housing committee have no plans at the moment for re-developing the site or offering it for industry, Ald Harold Lambert explained at a public meeting on Thursday.

Ald Lambert, chairman of the council's housing committee attended the meeting at Hillfoot School with Coun Roy Thwaites, Labour councillor for Owlerton, to answer queries from residents worried about the future of the area.

Coun Thwaites said afterwards that the main problem was access to the area.

"At present there is only one entrance by road, and that goes under a low bridge which would make it unsuitable for industrial development. I would be against a major housing re-development of the area while it is so inaccessible," he said.

The clearance programme will be going on in 1972-73 but meanwhile we shall pull down any individual properties that fall below standard. The occupants will be re-housed in other areas.

Good property in the area will be left standing and will not be affected under the present arrangement.

Coun Thwaites hopes that a plan will be drawn up for a larger development, taking in some of the surrounding area and including another entrance quarter of a mile away.

Indignant residents of Parkwood Springs, Sheffield—"the forgotten village within a city"—have formed a residents' action association.

The small community, of 1,000 just two miles from the city centre, has no bus services, doctor, post office or library.

Surrounded by large quarries, earthworks, a gasworks, tipping areas and a power station, with the Man-

chester - Sheffield railway running nearby, Parkwood Springs has only one access point.

The only way in — and out — is via Bardwell Road, under a low railway bridge just wide enough for one vehicle, which leads to a set of dead-end roads on a steep hillside.

The chairman of the residents' association, Mr George Ellis, of Pickering Road, said: "We know buses can get into Parkwood Springs because the public

RESIDENTS of a "forgotten village" want to put themselves on Sheffield city map. They form the 1,000-strong population of Parkwood Springs, less than two miles from the city centre.

A residents' action association has been launched to sort out problems in the area, bordering Neepsend, over which a redevelopment question-mark hangs. Councillors are being invited to a meeting to be held soon.

"We wonder how many people know where Parkwood Springs is," said association chairman Mr. George Ellis, of Pickering Road. "How many city councillors do, for that matter?"

Redevelopment is a long-standing problem. The area comes under 1972-3 plans, but not for housing purposes.

Coun. Roy Thwaites, of Owlerton, who believes that isolation is a barrier to attracting industry, said the area has yet to be fully programmed.

Uncertainty

"The uncertainty of what is going to happen to us, and when, creates a vast amount of problems in itself," pointed out Mr. Ellis.

"No private landlord is going to invest money in property repairs if he cannot see any returns, therefore houses fall into disrepair.

"Private owners have difficulty in selling property, and residents resent spending anything even on the interior of their homes."

A survey conducted by a group of students — which led to the association's formation — showed that Parkwood Springs consisted of 380 houses, mostly owned by private landlords.

About 100 are self-owned and 40 by Sheffield Corporation. Majority of residents have lived in the area for at least 20 years, some all their lives.

library bus gets in and so do coaches for fishing trips."

Coun Roy Thwaites, Labour representative for Owlerton Ward and chairman of the Transport Committee, said last night: "Single-decker buses would go under but drivers would have to be extra careful. The bridge is about 10ft 6ins at its highest and with buses 10ft, 3ins to 10ft 4ins there's not much space.

"During the week cars and lorries parked add extra difficulties. The public libraries bus is an older, smaller vehicle and doesn't have a schedule to keep to."

Mr Alfred Eadon, of Pickering Road, a committee member of the action group, said residents first tried to get a bus service 15 years ago.

He added: "Old people cannot leave the house because once they get to the bottom of the hill they can't get back.

"We wouldn't expect a service every five minutes and we will pay for it. People have to take taxis at 4s 6d. Even if they paid slightly over the odds for a bus service it would be cheaper than a taxi.

"Our relatives won't come and visit us because of the walk up the hill. Only people who live here will face the walk."

Mr Harry Carr, of Douglas Road, deputy chairman of the association, said it was only in the last few months they had had electric street lighting. Before that they had gas.

Mr Ellis said: "The major problem which has been with us for many years is that of redevelopment.

Explained

Coun Thwaites said he could not understand this as he and Ald Harold Lambert, chairman of the housing committee, had explained to residents only last week what the position was.

"There were no set plans for the area, he said, because of the isolation. Before any development for housing or light industry could be considered there would have to be access from another direction.

Mr Eadon, who was born at Parkwood Springs 45 years ago, can remember when there were over 600 houses. Now there are only 380.

Tipping area

Parkwood Springs is triangular-shaped, flanked by Sheffield-Manchester railway quarries and earthworks and a vast tipping area. Access is through steelworks via a low railway bridge.

Apart from redevelopment, recent difficulties have been fourfold, Mr. Ellis said. There are rehoused "problem" families in the village; hazards from demolished or empty houses; unauthorised tipping and wrecking of the only hall.

"We are determined to get some — if not all — our problems answered, not only by mere words and promises but by action," he pledged.

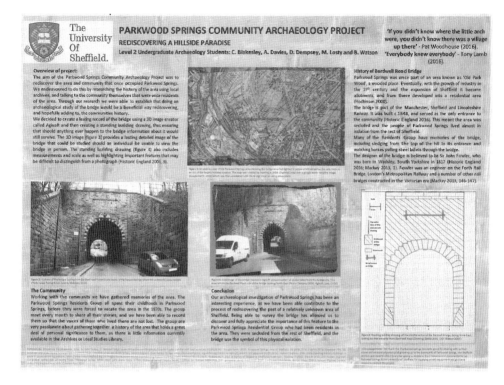

Full Circle
Present Day on Parkwood Springs
I revisited Parkwood Springs 14-03-2016

My first impression when I got under the railway arch was all the industry that had grown at the bottom of Douglas Road, Wallace Road, and Vale Road. Douglas Road is buried under the burnt out ski slope and wild flowers are taking over the landscape.
Trees are also growing all around the hillside as in the 1800s.

Further up the hill on Wallace Road, Pickering Road and Mount Road, caravans are all around everywhere. A large fence has been erected all around them.

I wanted to see what it was like for the people living up there in the 21st century.
What brought them to Parkwood Springs and why?

At the present time there are no street lights, Electricity, Water or Sanitation, but many people are choosing to live there in caravans.

I spoke to a very nice chap who was willing to tell me how he came to live there.
He lives alone in his caravan and has fixed himself up with a generator for electricity a battery for his radio and has a log burner in his van for heating. He cooks with gas and

gets the large gas bottles delivered.   He likes to keep things tidy.
He works for himself as landscape gardener, painter decorator and told me he could not afford to live in a house with high rents, because after all his expenses were paid there would be nothing left for anything else.
I saw some solar panels that people have installed for themselves.

Most of the people are in some kind of paid work, with occupations as follows.
Engineer,
HGV driver,
Music teacher of autistic people,
Train caterer on the London line.
Some people are on zero hours contracts.
They can be asked by these work agencies to go into work at a moment's notice, or told there are no jobs at all.
However they manage in that sort of situation is anyone's guess.
They are penalised if they join more than one work agency.
This is sounding more like the 1920s rather than the 21st century.

Someone goes to the supermarkets last thing after closing time to get food from the bins of the very wasteful supermarkets of today.   Good food that is thrown away to go to land fill. One woman living in a caravan has three sons who go school; they enjoy playing all around Parkwood Springs just like we did long ago.

Some of the young men who live there have never bothered to vote in an election, but are now thinking more about voting at the next election since Jeremy Corbyn got in as the leader of the labour party, someone at last who is prepared to do more for the poorer people of our society.

Acknowledgments

A BIG THANK YOU to all my family and friends for putting up with me and all the ear bashing I have given them while writing this, you all know who you are, especially my husband for all his help and support.
Barbara Lee (nee Pierce) for all her encouragement.
Peter Addison for photos and excerpts from "Parkwood Springs Echo"
Ana Anastasio archaeology student for the 2014 Photos.
Students of Archaeology Study of the Railway Arch. "The University of Sheffield" 2016
Mel and Joan Jones for all their sound advice and know how.
Sheffield Local Studies Library, Archives.
Historic England.
Sheffield News Papers Telegraph and Star.
Donald Alexander for excerpts from his book "Orreight Me Ol`"
Paul Hodkinson for excerpts from his book "A History of Neepsend"
"Morning Star "News Paper for excerpts on the ski Slope.
"Copper Beech Studios" for Photographs.
I would like to thank all the past residents who have allowed me to add their stories and photos to this book. Without them this book would not have been written.

Sadly in 2016 Allan Cottingham passed away.
And Connie Walters can no longer be contacted by phone.